Edizione 2018
COMPUTER BASED

Francesca Basile
Jacopo D'Andria Ursoleo
Claire Moore

Verso le Prove NAZIONALI

Scuola Secondaria di Primo Grado

Inglese

ELI PUBLISHING

Indice

file audio mp3 per tutti i brani e i *Listening Tests*.

Verso le Prove nazionali – Inglese
di F. Basile, J. D'Andria Ursoleo, C. Moore
nuova edizione ampliata

Responsabile editoriale: Beatrice Loreti
Responsabile di produzione: Francesco Capitano
Progetto grafico e impaginazione: Airone Comunicazione - Enea Ciccarelli
Copertina: Curvilinee
Foto: Shutterstock
Consulenza didattica: Tiziana Sampaolesi

Via Brecce – Loreto
tel. 071 750 701
info@elilaspigaedizioni.it
www.elilaspigaedizioni.it

Stampato in Italia presso
Tecnostampa - Pigini Group Printing Division - Loreto - Trevi
17.83.346.2
ISBN 978-88-468-3699-1

INTRODUZIONE

L'opera si propone di preparare gli studenti del triennio della Scuola Secondaria di Primo Grado alla nuova Prova nazionale di Inglese in versione mista: *Computer Based* (CB) o cartacea.

Si articola in due volumi, uno per i docenti e uno per gli studenti.

Il volume per gli studenti è composto da:

- una **prima prova con soluzione guidata** (***Practice Test with Tips***) che fornisce commenti e strategie per risolvere i quesiti; questo permetterà allo studente di comprendere ciò che viene richiesto e di trovare le risposte adeguate.
- Otto **prove propedeutiche** (***Practice Tests***), strutturate a partire dal modello delle prove Invalsi di Italiano e della Certificazione Linguistica *Cambridge English: Key* (QCER A2), tarate su tre livelli di difficoltà crescente (*easy – medium – difficult*) che avvicineranno l'alunno alle diverse tipologie testuali previste, facendo prendere confidenza con i linguaggi e le caratteristiche di ognuna.
- Al termine di ogni prova, una **tabella** consente agli alunni di registrare i loro risultati al fine di riconoscere il proprio livello di preparazione e di **autovalutarsi**.
- L'ampia sezione di *Listening* è stata impostata sul modello della certificazione linguistica *Cambridge English*: *Key* (QCER A2) e comprende 6 test, due per ogni livello di difficoltà del libro. Ciascun test è suddiviso a sua volta in 5 sezioni corrispondenti alle seguenti tipologie di esercizi:
  - *Three-option multiple choice* (**risposta multipla**)
  - *Matching* (**abbinamento** basato sull'ascolto di un dialogo)
  - *Three-option multiple choice* (**scelta multipla** per ricercare un'informazione specifica)
  - *Gap-fill* (**completamento**)

  Tutti gli audio sono stati registrati da speaker madrelingua.
- Una sezione speciale intitolata "**Grammar Reference** e **Verb Tables**" che guiderà gli studenti a conoscere e a ripassare le parti di grammatica presenti nelle prove Invalsi.

Nella Sezione Docente del sito web (www.elilaspigaedizioni.it/invalsionline) sono disponibili le *Answer Keys* e i *Tapescripts* di ciascun test. Sul sito della casa editrice inoltre è fornito il file audio mp3 dei brani proposti in ogni prova.

Il volume per i docenti contiene indicazioni didattiche sulle competenze di lettura e sulle principali funzioni linguistiche che vengono esercitate nei test, oltre alle griglie di correzione e alle soluzioni di tutti i quesiti.

Section 1 – READING SKILLS

Part 1 | Questions A1 – A5

*Leggi con attenzione i seguenti brevi messaggi. Cosa dicono? Per ciascun quesito, scegli la risposta corretta (***A***,* **B** *oppure* **C***) in base a ciò che hai letto. Ti viene fornito un esempio (***0***) all'inizio.*

TIPS

In questa parte trovi piccoli cartelli che riproducono dei sintetici avvisi pubblicati dalle scuole, stazioni ferroviarie, aeroporti, negozi, ristoranti, uffici o altri posti pubblici, organizzazioni, segnali stradali o testi molto brevi. La domanda ti chiede *Che cosa dice il cartello?* oppure *Il messaggio dice che...* quindi devi leggere il messaggio o il cartello attentamente per poi passare alle tre opzioni sulla destra. Nel caso il cartello o il messaggio contengano dei termini che non conosci cerca di intuirne il significato dal contesto. Ti puoi allenare leggendo articoli di giornali e periodici, pubblicità, brochure turistiche, istruzioni, ricette. Il messaggio dell'esempio dice *NEVER LEAVE LUGGAGE UNATTENDED!* che vuol dire *Non lasciare mai il bagaglio incustodito*. Questo non vuol dire che i passeggeri devono portar via il proprio bagaglio quando partono (*Passengers must remember their own luggage when they leave*) o che non dovrebbero lasciare qualcun altro a guardia del bagaglio (*Passengers cannot let someone else look after their luggage*) ma che dovrebbero sempre stare con il loro bagaglio (*Passengers must stay with their own luggage at all times*). Fai sempre attenzione alle frasi positive o negative.

Example

0

Passengers:

A. ☐ must remember their own luggage when they leave.

B. ☒ must stay with their own luggage at all times.

C. ☐ cannot let someone else look after their luggage.

A1. The advertisement says the computer game:

A. ☐ is only suitable for families.

B. ☐ does not work on the seller's own PC.

C. ☐ is in excellent condition and almost new.

From: Jacopo
To: Beatrice

Hi Bea! Have you remembered about the golf club trip? We have to tell Francesca if we are interested and I wanted to know if you are going.

Jac

A2. Jacopo wrote this email to Beatrice:

A. ☐ to check if Beatrice is going on the trip.

B. ☐ to ask Beatrice to book three seats on the trip.

C. ☐ to remind Beatrice about the date of the trip.

NOTICE

Sunday's swimming competition starts at 5.30 pm. Please arrive at least two hours before for swimming practice.

A3. Which of the following statements is correct?

A. ☐ The notice says that there is an opportunity to swim before the competition.

B. ☐ The notice says that all swimmers should get some practice before Sunday.

C. ☐ The notice says that the swimming competition lasts for two hours.

Text Message

Alejandra, we are outside the theatre. Text me if you are going to be late tonight and we'll see the next play. If you are not coming, we'll go in now.

Johannes

A4. Alejandra should:

A. ☐ wait for Johannes inside the theatre.

B. ☐ tell Johannes which play she wants to watch.

C. ☐ let Johannes know if she is delayed.

ATTENTION!

Remember to throw away any remaining medicine within two months of opening this bottle.

A5. Which of the following statements is correct?

A. ☐ Throw away unopened bottles of medicine within two months.

B. ☐ You can use this medicine up to two months after opening it.

C. ☐ The bottle contains enough medicine for two months.

Part 2 | Questions A6 – A10

Leggi con attenzione le seguenti definizioni di alcuni termini. Qual è il termine corrispondente a ciascuna definizione? Associa le definizioni **A6 – A10** *con i termini* **A – G**. *Ci sono due termini extra, che non avrai bisogno di utilizzare.*

TIPS

In questa parte troverai definizioni di mestieri, animali, cibo, cose che si possono trovare in una casa, vestiti, oggetti della scuola, parti del corpo, ecc. Per esempio *può essere trovato in una cucina*. Nella pagina trovi un elenco di sette vocaboli, due dei quali non corrispondono ad alcuna definizione. Se la definizione inizia con *It is...* dovrai cercare un oggetto o un animale. Se la definizione inizia con *A person who...* la soluzione sarà il nome di un mestiere o di un'azione che riguarda le persone. Per allenarti puoi raggruppare i termini in aree lessicali, come per esempio gli oggetti della scuola o i vestiti, e annotarli in un quaderno per aiutarti ad ampliare il tuo vocabolario d'inglese.

A6. ☐ A person who designs buildings.

A7. ☐ It helps us measure or draw straight lines.

A8. ☐ A person who is walking in the street, but not travelling in a vehicle.

A9. ☐ It has wings, but it can't fly.

A10. ☐ A person who repairs and installs tubes, fixtures and water pipes.

A. Waiter.

B. Pedestrian.

C. Architect.

D. Ruler.

E. Firefighter.

F. Plumber.

G. Ostrich.

Part 3 | Questions A11 – A15

*Leggi con attenzione le seguenti cinque brevi conversazioni. Per ciascuna di esse, scegli poi il completamento corretto (***A***,* **B** *oppure* **C***) in base a ciò che hai letto. Ti viene fornito un esempio (***0***) all'inizio.*

TIPS

Questa parte contiene cinque domande che si riferiscono a brevi conversazioni. La prima persona dice qualcosa e tu devi scegliere fra tre possibili risposte. Per trovare quella giusta, devi pensare a ciò che la seconda persona direbbe normalmente in questa situazione. Quando si esegue questa parte, conviene prima leggere tutte le frasi e tutte le possibili risposte. A volte la prima frase ti aiuterà a scegliere la risposta corretta. A volte sarà la frase dopo. Devi prestare molta attenzione per esempio agli avverbi che descrivono dove, quando, come, perché si compie un'azione. Gli avverbi interrogativi *why*, *where*, *how* e *when* si collocano all'inizio di una frase interrogativa, alla quale si può rispondere con un'altra frase o con una frase introdotta da una preposizione. Per esempio la domanda *Where do you come from?* dell'esempio iniziale chiede da quale città provieni, e non da quale luogo stai arrivando.

Example

0

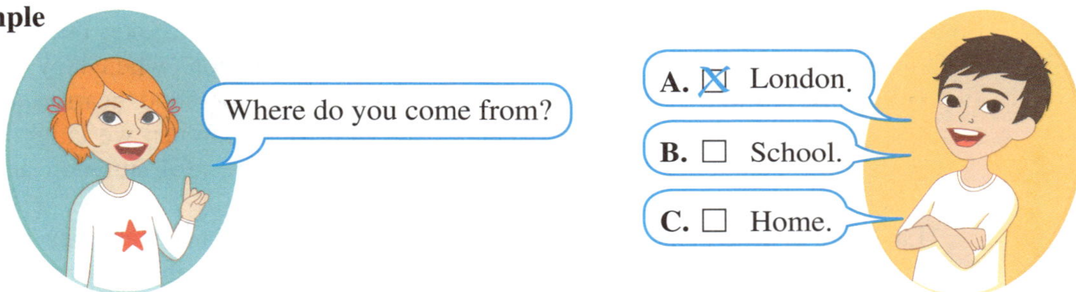

A11. Excuse me, Sir, can I help you?

A. ☐ I've got them.
B. ☐ Yes, please!
C. ☐ No, I haven't.

A12. Matthew, where's your History book?

A. ☐ It's £15.00.
B. ☐ I forgot it.
C. ☐ Yes, it is.

A13. Shall we play football this afternoon?

A. ☐ All right.
B. ☐ No, it's not here.
C. ☐ If you'd like to.

A14. Are you coming to Linda's party tomorrow?

A. ☐ I don't know yet.
B. ☐ Sorry, I haven't.
C. ☐ I am on my way.

A15. How long have you been studying English?

A. ☐ Quite early.
B. ☐ For two years now.
C. ☐ It isn't enough.

Part 4 | Questions A16 – A25

*Leggi con attenzione il brano seguente e le relative domande. Per ciascun quesito, scegli poi la risposta corretta (***A***,* **B***,* **C** *oppure* **D***) in base a ciò che hai letto.*

Prima di svolgere gli esercizi, leggi i Tips *a pagina 9.*

Don't make me laugh!

'**Laughing** is the best medicine.' We don't know if this is true, but we definitely feel better after laughing. But why do we laugh? Every laugh is so personal that it is like our own **signature**. Everybody can laugh without learning how to. We learn how to speak, but not how to laugh. Little babies can laugh long before they are able to speak. Some researchers **claim** that genetic factors determine the way we laugh. There was the case of two twins who were separated at birth and who lived with different families, but who were then reunited as adults. They discovered that they had a lot in common, including the same laugh.

We do not decide when to laugh, it's a natural impulse, and it's very difficult to fake laughing; even if people think that we laugh after hearing a joke, but this is not the main reason. A study has revealed that people laugh more when they are in social situations. It is true that we also laugh when we are alone, but loud, hearty and sometimes uncontrollable laughter occurs when we are with friends. When we laugh, we connect with other people. It helps to **ease** the tension in a stressful situation and provokes positive feelings.

Laughing is contagious, like **yawning**; this creates a stronger human connection between people. The area of the brain that controls laughing is deep inside it and it is very far from the area responsible for language and memory. It is probably for this reason that we cannot stop laughing even when it is inappropriate.

Some therapists say that laughing is not only good for the soul, but also for the body, because our muscles relax and we feel better when we laugh. Laughing is like jogging – our **lungs** get clearer, our appetite increases and our circulation is also stimulated. Now many doctors **agree** that laughter has various important benefits for our health.

Dr Adams, whose nickname is Patch, is an American doctor who cures his patients with unconventional methods. He sometimes dresses as a clown and then visits young patients to make them laugh. When a movie based on the doctor's career (called *Patch Adams*) was **released**, the doctor didn't like it. He said that he was represented only as a funny doctor, while his studies about humour were very serious.

However, laughing has not always been a positive or healthy activity.

In the past, **tickling** was used as a method of torture. The feet of the torture victim were **tied** and covered with salt, then a **goat** started **licking** them to provoke laughter in the victim. In this case, we cannot say that the victim enjoyed laughing very much!

GLOSSARY

to laugh (v) ridere
signature (n) firma, segno distintivo
to claim (v) sostenere
to ease (v) allentare
to yawn (v) sbadigliare
lung (n) polmone
to agree (v) essere d'accordo
to release (v) lanciare
to tickle (v) fare il solletico
to tie (v) legare
goat (n) capra
to lick (v) leccare

TIPS

Nella parte 4 trovi un testo lungo, seguito da una serie di esercizi di comprensione. Non leggere il testo in maniera frettolosa. Quando leggi il brano presta attenzione all'argomento principale, ma anche ai vocaboli o ai dettagli che possono assumere o meno una certa importanza. Per capire quali informazioni sono più importanti all'interno del testo, il suggerimento principale è quello di leggere le domande prima del brano per poter trovare nel testo le risposte corrette. Ti consigliamo di sottolineare le frasi o i termini più importanti durante la lettura in modo da non perdere tempo quando cercherai di dare una soluzione definitiva agli esercizi, le affermazioni vere o false, la parte mancante in una frase, la definizione di una parola o di un'espressione. La richiesta fornisce spesso l'indicazione del rigo o dei righi dove l'informazione può essere trovata. Per esempio il termine *joke* fa riferimento al rigo 10 dove leggiamo *We do not decide when to laugh, it is a natural impulse and it is very difficult to fake laughing* (*Non decidiamo quando ridere, è un impulso naturale ed è molto difficile fare una risata finta*) quindi la corretta soluzione è **C**: *something said to make people laugh* (*qualcosa detta per far ridere le persone*).

A16. According to the text, babies can laugh:

A. ☒ before they are able to speak.
B. ☐ after they are able to speak.
C. ☐ when they become able to speak.
D. ☐ if and only if they are able to speak.

A17. Are the following statements **true** or **false**? Tick as appropriate.

		True	**False**
a	People can change their natural laugh.		X
b	Everyone's laugh is similar.		X
c	People have different laughs.	X	

A18. There was the case of two twins who were separated at birth and who lived with different families, but who were then reunited as adults, and had a lot in common, including the same:

laugh ....

A19. The term 'joke' (line 10) means:

A. ☐ a ridiculous phrase.
B. ☐ a game to play together.
C. ☒ something said to make people laugh.
D. ☐ a story.

A20. According to the text, we laugh more:

A. ☐ when we are alone.
B. ☒ when we are with other people.
C. ☐ when we are at home.
D. ☐ when we listen to a joke.

A21. The expression 'laughing is contagious' (line 16) means:

A. ☐ it is not possible to communicate it to other people.
B. ☐ it causes a different reaction in other people.
C. ☒ it is so irresistible that other people start doing the same thing.
D. ☐ it is so annoying that other people start doing the same thing.

A22. According to the text, which of the following is not one of the benefits of laughing?

A. ☐ Developing a good appetite.
B. ☐ Feeling relaxed.
C. ☒ Yawning.
D. ☐ Developing a good connection with people around you.

A23. Why does the article compare laughing with jogging?

A. ☐ Because you don't feel hungry after it.
B. ☐ Because you don't need to move your muscles.
C. ☐ Because everybody likes jogging.
D. ☐ Because it is a good exercise.

A24. Dr Adams:

A. ☐ thought that the movie *Patch Adams* was based on his life.
B. ☐ thought that the movie *Patch Adams* was an invention of the director.
C. ☐ thought that the movie *Patch Adams* gave an incorrect idea of his work.
D. ☐ thought that the movie *Patch Adams* was very good.

A25. The text describes a form of tickling torture. Why was the torture so painful?

A. ☐ Because the goat was tied down.
B. ☐ Because the victim could not move while the goat licked his feet.
C. ☐ Because the victim enjoyed being tickled.
D. ☐ Because the goat didn't like the salt.

Part 5 | Questions A26 – A35

Leggi con attenzione il brano seguente sui mezzi di trasporto a Londra. Indica poi se le affermazioni **A26** – **A35** *sono vere 'True'* (**A**), *false 'False'* (**B**) *o non menzionate dal testo 'Doesn't say'* (**C**).

Prima di svolgere gli esercizi, leggi i Tips *a pagina 12.*

Getting around London

Daily Travelcard prices		
Anytime	Zones 1-4	£12.20
Anytime	Zones 1-6	£17.00
Off-peak (after 9.30 am)	Zones 1-6	£12.00
Off-peak (after 9.30 am)	Zones 1-9	£12.80

Tourists from all over the world can easily **get around** in London thanks to many transport options. London is among the biggest cities in Europe, and it has one of the world's largest public transport systems. That's why many Londoners don't need to own a car. Public transport includes buses, suburban trains, the Docklands Light Railway (DLR), and most importantly the underground, called the Tube which, with its nine lines, represents one of the easiest and most comprehensive ways of moving around the city.

London's public transport system provides transport for people who live and work in the city. It is not advantageous for people buying single tickets. If you want to visit London, it is best to buy one of the different passes or cards available. Prices for using the system depend on how far you travel and what zones you enter into. If you live in London, or even if you're just visiting for a few days, the cheapest method of travel is to take out an Oyster Card. You can buy these cards online or at a station, they are free, and you recharge them online or at any tube station.

If people travel into London from outside the city, they may take the train or a bus! Traffic is **jammed** in the British capital, and the central streets have paid access. Parking is expensive. Daily travelcards can be used on buses, underground trains, suburban trains and the Docklands Light Railway. If you add a travelcard to the London Pass, you will get free use of public transport included in your Pass, as well as free access to lots of attractions. For example, if you consider travelcards for zones 1-4 they include tourist destinations such as Wembley, Wimbledon, the 02 Arena, Greenwich and London City Airport. Moreover, for people travelling together, taxis will often be cheaper than buying single-journey tube tickets for the underground.

GLOSSARY

to get around (v) muoversi, spostarsi

jammed (a) congestionato

TIPS

Nella parte 5 troverai un testo non continuo associato a una tabella o a un grafico. Si tratta di un testo adattato da articoli di giornale e riviste. Le domande in questa parte possono essere di comprensione, a scelta multipla (con tre opzioni) e viene chiesto di decidere se, secondo il testo, le affermazioni sono corrette (**True**), sbagliate (**False**), o se non vi sono informazioni sufficienti nel testo (**Doesn't say**). Dopo aver letto attentamente il testo, leggi le affermazioni che si trovano sotto il testo e vai a rileggere quella parte dove si trova quell'informazione. Per esempio la domanda 26 dice *London has the world's second largest public transport system*. Nei primi due righi del testo leggiamo *London is among the biggest cities in Europe, and it has one of the world's largest public transport systems*. Ma non c'è scritto da nessuna parte che Londra ha il secondo più grande sistema di trasporto pubblico del mondo. Una o due affermazioni saranno legate al grafico associato al testo, per esempio la frase 28 afferma *A London daily Travel card costs £ 12.20 in Zone 6 at 8 o'clock* ma nella tabella leggiamo che quel prezzo corrisponde alla carta giornaliera nelle zone 1-4 a tutte le ore.

A26. London has the world's second largest public transport system.
A. ☐ true **B.** ☐ false **C.** ☐ doesn't say

A27. The underground in London is also called the Tube.
A. ☐ true **B.** ☐ false **C.** ☐ doesn't say

A28. A London daily travelcard costs £12.20 in Zone 6 at 8 o'clock.
A. ☐ true **B.** ☐ false **C.** ☐ doesn't say

A29. London's public transport can be very cheap if you buy one ticket at a time.
A. ☐ true **B.** ☐ false **C.** ☐ doesn't say

A30. You can travel by train or by bus to get into London from outside the city.
A. ☐ true **B.** ☐ false **C.** ☐ doesn't say

A31. Oyster cards may be used to travel the Docklands Light Railway.
A. ☐ true **B.** ☐ false **C.** ☐ doesn't say

A32. You can't visit Greenwich Observatory after 6 pm.
A. ☐ true **B.** ☐ false **C.** ☐ doesn't say

A33. If you want to save money, you could add a travelcard to the London Pass.
A. ☐ true **B.** ☐ false **C.** ☐ doesn't say

A34. When you buy a London Pass and Travel, you can enter many attractions.
A. ☐ true **B.** ☐ false **C.** ☐ doesn't say

A35. It's better to share a taxi fare with at least three other people.
A. ☐ true **B.** ☐ false **C.** ☐ doesn't say

Section 2 – USE OF ENGLISH

Part 1 | Questions B1 – B5

*Leggi con attenzione il brano seguente su una gita a Nottingham. Per ciascuno spazio, scegli poi il giusto completamento (**A**, **B**, oppure **C**) in base a ciò che hai letto. Ti viene fornito un esempio (**0**) all'inizio del testo.*

TIPS

La parte 1 della sezione *Use of English* testa la conoscenza delle strutture grammaticali e il loro uso corretto nei vari contesti. I brani sono adattati da articoli di quotidiani o riviste, o altri testi autentici. Alcune parole sono state cancellate dal testo e la parola mancante va scelta fra tre opzioni. Gli elementi mancanti possono essere verbi, articoli, pronomi, preposizioni, collocazioni, frasi idiomatiche, verbi fraseologici e congiunzioni. È meglio leggere tutto il testo per poi decidere qual è la parte mancante. Per esempio l'esempio **0** chiede di completare la frase *On my last holidays I went (0) _____ Nottingham with all my family* con le opzioni *along*, *to* oppure *from*. L'opzione corretta è **B** perché la preposizione *to* indica un movimento verso un luogo determinato, mentre *along* indica un movimento lineare lungo un fiume, una strada e non verso un luogo; mentre *from* indica una provenienza da un luogo o l'origine.

Example

0	**A.** ☐ along	**B.** ☒ to	**C.** ☐ from

A trip to Nottingham

On my last holidays I went (**0**) ………… Nottingham with all my family. Nottingham is famous all over the world for the legend (**B1**) ………… Robin Hood. The tales of Robin Hood have been passed down from generation to generation. There were tour guides wearing old costumes and telling the story of Robin. Robin Hood is widely known as a highly skilled archer, a swordsman and a good-natured thief who travelled through Sherwood Forest in the county of Nottinghamshire stealing from the rich and giving to the poor, assisted (**B2**) ………… a group of criminals known as his Merry Men, and for this reason he has become the symbol of the county.

We visited the Castle, which was used by the Sheriff of Nottingham (**B3**) ………… a court. Did you know that there is still a Sheriff of Nottingham? My brother took a picture of me next to the statue of Robin Hood, and then we walked to the Old Market Square, right in the centre of the town.

There was a beautiful ferris wheel (**B4**) ………… the square. We took a ride on it and saw the city from the top. It was amazing. We had lunch in a fast food restaurant near the square and then we did (**B5**) ………… shopping. I bought a green Robin Hood hoodie for my friend Thomas and a Nottingham T-shirt for me. After lunch we went to the Nottingham Industrial Museum, where we saw a lot of things, from motorbikes to telephones, steam powered tractors to 13th century clocks.

I had a great time in Nottingham!

B1.	**A.** ☐ of	**B.** ☐ with	**C.** ☐ that
B2.	**A.** ☐ by	**B.** ☐ up	**C.** ☐ with
B3.	**A.** ☐ as	**B.** ☐ on	**C.** ☐ by
B4.	**A.** ☐ to	**B.** ☐ in	**C.** ☐ at
B5.	**A.** ☐ the	**B.** ☐ a	**C.** ☐ some

Part 2 | Questions B6 – B15

Leggi con attenzione il brano seguente, poi scrivi la parola mancante in ciascuno spazio. Scrivi solo UNA parola per ciascuno spazio. Ti viene fornito un esempio (**0**) *all'inizio del testo.*

TIPS

Nella parte 2 bisogna completare un testo bucato, senza avere delle opzioni. A prima vista può risultare difficile ma poi basta seguire il filo del discorso e tenere presente che di solito gli elementi mancanti possono essere forme verbali, articoli, pronomi, preposizioni e congiunzioni. Attenzione alla frase che precede lo spazio vuoto! È meglio leggere tutto il testo per poi decidere qual è la parte mancante.
Nell'esempio **0** troviamo *Did you ever dream, for example, (0) ____ climbing Mount Everest or visiting Antarctica?* Dove la parte mancante è la preposizione *of* perché il verbo *dream of* si usa per parlare di obiettivi o aspirazioni, in questo caso scalare il monte Everest o visitare l'Antartico.

Adventures of a lifetime!

What is better than an adventure to escape from your daily routine? Did you ever dream, for example, (**0**) .... climbing Mount Everest or visiting Antarctica? (**B6**) .... so, you're not the only one! Every year, a lot of people try to climb the world's highest mountains or walk across continents.

(**B7**) .... the past, explorers used different tools such as compasses and maps, whereas modern adventurers have at their disposal satellite phones and GPS to get to destination and enjoy the wonders of those places. Voyagers also use their travel experiences (**B8**) .... let the world have knowledge or information (**B9**) .... climate change and help people in the countries they visit. Let's have a look (**B10**) .... one of the 21st-century's memorable adventures.

Ed Stafford is a forty-year old man (**B11**) .... the UK and he is the first person who managed to walk the length of the Amazon River. He started from a small river in the Andes mountains of Peru and arrived at the river's mouth in Brazil, twenty-six months later. Ed was bitten by ants and mosquitoes every day (**B12**) .... luckily he didn't meet big and dangerous animals like snakes, crocodiles and jaguars. During his trip, Ed had (**B13**) .... get food every single day. Sometimes he had a lot of difficulty in finding fruit, nuts, fish and that's why Ed often felt weak and hungry.

Technology was fundamental to Ed's survival. The radio was very useful to ask local people (**B14**) .... food and permission to enter their land. Many of them came to meet him and spontaneously offer to guide him through the impenetrable rainforest. During his walking, Ed wrote (**B15**) .... blog about his daily experiences. Through his walk Ed let the world know more about climate change, and environmental problems in Brazil and Peru.

Section 3 – GRAMMAR KNOWLEDGE

Questions C1 – C10

Leggi con attenzione e rispondi ai seguenti quesiti di riflessione sulla lingua inglese.

C1. Complete the following sentence with the correct form of the verbs in brackets: present simple or present continuous?

Hi Sarah! __________ (*to be*) you free on Sunday evening? Sue and I __________ (*to go*) to the shopping centre… Would you like to join us?

TIPS

Il present simple indica un'azione abituale, mentre il present continuous esprime un'azione che si sta compiendo in questo momento. Nella prima frase l'espressione di tempo *on Sunday evening* ci fa capire che si tratta di un'azione abituale. Inoltre il verbo *to be* non può essere usato al present continuous.

C2. Complete the space in the following sentence appropriately: 'Dad __________ cooks dinner.'

A. ☐ tomorrow
B. ☐ sometimes
C. ☐ tonight
D. ☐ now

TIPS

La frase *Dad* __________ *cooks dinner* è coniugata al present simple e dato che è un'azione abituale dobbiamo scegliere un avverbio di frequenza (*sometimes*) mentre le altre tre opzioni sono avverbi di tempo.

C3. Which of the following sentences is grammatically correct?

A. ☐ Justin will be stayed with his aunt this week.
B. ☐ Justin did stayed with his aunt this week.
C. ☐ Justin is staying with his aunt this week.
D. ☐ Justin stays with his aunt this week.

TIPS

L'opzione **A** *Justin will be stayed with his aunt this week* non è corretta perché *will be* indica un tempo futuro mentre il verbo *stayed* è un participio passato. L'opzione **B** *Justin did stayed with his aunt this week* non è corretta perché *stayed* è già coniugato al passato e quindi non è necessario aggiungere l'ausiliare *did*. L'opzione **D** *Justin stays with his aunt this week* non è corretta perché il verbo *stays* si riferisce a un'azione abituale mentre l'espressione *this week* si riferisce a un arco di tempo ben definito. Quindi, l'opzione corretta è la **C**: *Justin is staying with his aunt this week.*

C4. Complete the following sentences by deleting the incorrect option.

A. They would love *to go/going* to the theatre tonight with their friends.

B. Would you like *to rent/renting* a car?

C. Alex hates *listening/listened* to heavy metal music. Do you?

TIPS

I verbi *hate, love, like,* e *prefer* sono generalmente seguiti da un gerundio quando il senso è generale, e dall'infinito quando si riferiscono a una situazione particolare. L'uso dell'infinito è obbligatorio con le espressioni *would love to, would like to, would hate to.*

C5. Complete the space in the following sentence appropriately: 'Coco Chanel ________ from France.'

A. ☐ have been

B. ☐ weren't

C. ☐ was

D. ☐ has been

TIPS

Per capire quale verbo manca nella frase *Coco Chanel* __________ *from France*, possiamo escludere subito *weren't* (**B**) perché il soggetto della frase Coco Chanel è una terza persona singolare (**she**), mentre *weren't* si usa con i soggetti *we/you/they*. Il simple past è usato per descrivere un evento che è iniziato e finito nel passato mentre il present perfect descrive eventi accaduti in un momento non specificato. Dato che parliamo di un personaggio del passato dobbiamo usare il simple past e quindi *was*.

C6. Complete the spaces in the following sentence appropriately: 'Jennifer __________ at home any more. She __________ to live on her own three months ago.'

A. ☐ isn't living; went

B. ☐ isn't living; has gone

C. ☐ hasn't been living; has gone

D. ☐ was going; went

TIPS

Nella frase *Jennifer* __________ *at home any more. She* __________ *to live on her own three months ago*, la presenza di *any more* (*non più*) ti fa capire che nella prima parte ci vuole un verbo al presente mentre nella seconda parte l'espressione *three months ago* ci fa scegliere l'opzione con il simple past. (Opzione **A**: *isn't living; went*)

C7. Complete the spaces in the following sentence appropriately: 'I did the __________ and __________ the kitchen.'

A. ☐ washed-up; tidied

B. ☐ washing-up; tidyed

C. ☐ washing-up; tidied

D. ☐ washing-up; tidyied

TIPS

Nella frase *I did the* __________ and __________ *the kitchen*, puoi tranquillamente escludere le opzioni **B** e **D** perché lo spelling del verbo *tidy* al passato è sbagliato (*tidyied* o *tidyed* anziché *tidied*). L'opzione corretta è la **C** perché lavare i piatti in inglese si dice *to do the washing-up* mentre il verbo *did* nella prima parte fa capire che la frase è al simple past.

C8. Complete the spaces in the following sentence appropriately: 'Mum, I'm going __________ the museum this evening __________ my friend Jane. I'm sorry that you can't come __________ me.'

A. ☐ to; with; with

B. ☐ along; with; after

C. ☐ in; with; with

D. ☐ for; after; with

TIPS

Nella frase *Mum, I'm going ______ the museum this evening _____ my friend Jane. I'm sorry that you can't come ________ me*, bisogna scegliere l'opzione con le preposizioni giuste. L'opzione corretta è la **A** (*to*; *with*; *with*) perché la preposizione *to* indica uno spostamento verso un luogo mentre la preposizione *with* traduce CON nel senso di insieme a.

C9. Complete the spaces in the following sentence appropriately: 'Let's buy a __________of tomatoes, __________ lettuce, __________ cucumber and… do we have __________ potatoes?'

A. ☐ kilo; some; a; any

B. ☐ ounce; some; a; some

C. ☐ bowl; any; a; some

D. ☐ bowl; some; an; any

TIPS

Nella frase *Let's buy a______of tomatoes, _______ lettuce, ________ cucumber and... do we have __________ potatoes*? L'opzione corretta è la **A** (*kilo*; *some*; *a*; *any*) in quanto non è possibile utilizzare *a/an* con i sostantivi non numerabili come *lettuce,* ma si può usare con i numerabili come *cucumber*. Per esprimere la quantità di un sostantivo non numerabile si usano espressioni come *some*, *a lot of*, *much*, *a bit of*, oppure una misura esatta come *a cup of, a bag of, 1 kg of, 1 L of*. Nella domanda *do we have _____ potatoes*? Si usa *any* perché *some* si usa solo nelle affermazioni o nelle offerte.

C10. Complete the space in the following sentence appropriately: 'Before George came to Britain, he ____________________ much English.'

A. ☐ couldn't understand

B. ☐ doesn't understand

C. ☐ can't understand

D. ☐ do understand

TIPS

Dato che la frase *Before George came to Britain, he ____________________ much English* è al passato (*came*) dobbiamo escludere le opzioni **B, C** e **D**, che contengono verbi al presente *doesn't understand - can't understand - do understand,* quindi l'unica scelta valida è la **A** (*couldn't understand*).

Ho trovato la prova: ☐ Difficile ☐ Più semplice di quanto pensassi ☐ Adeguata alle mie aspettative e capacità ☐ Altro

Section 1 – READING SKILLS

Part 1 | Questions A1 – A5

*Leggi con attenzione i seguenti brevi messaggi. Cosa dicono? Per ciascun quesito, scegli la risposta corretta (***A***,* **B** *oppure* **C***) in base a ciò che hai letto. Ti viene fornito un esempio (***0***) all'inizio.*

Example

0

Passengers:

A. ☐ must remember their own luggage when they leave.

B. ☒ must stay with their own luggage at all times.

C. ☐ cannot let someone else look after their luggage.

A1. The store is going to:

A. ☐ open later than normal on Thursday morning.

B. ☐ close from 10 am for staff training.

C. ☐ interview new staff on Thursday morning.

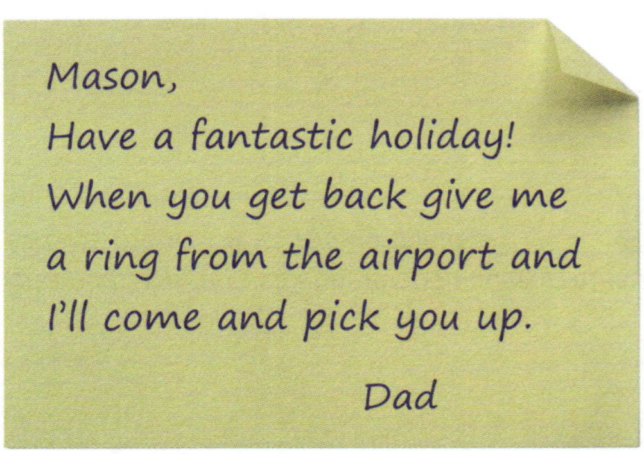

A2. The note says that:

A. ☐ Mason's father is offering to go and get Mason from the airport.

B. ☐ Mason's father wants to be picked up from the airport.

C. ☐ Mason's father has agreed to take Mason to the airport.

A3. Which of the following statements is correct?

A. ☐ It is possible to borrow DVDs in addition to six books.

B. ☐ The maximum number of books or DVDs you are allowed is six.

C. ☐ When returning books or CDs, your library card is needed.

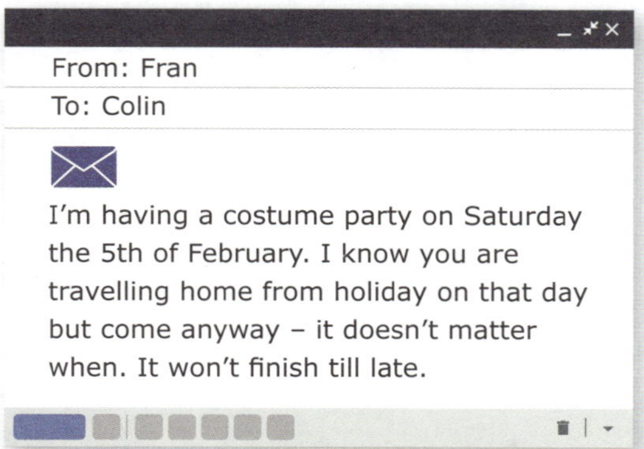

A4. Fran:

A. ☐ is asking Colin to get back as soon as he can on Sunday.

B. ☐ is inviting Colin to come to a party before he goes on holiday.

C. ☐ wants Colin to come to the party at whatever time he can.

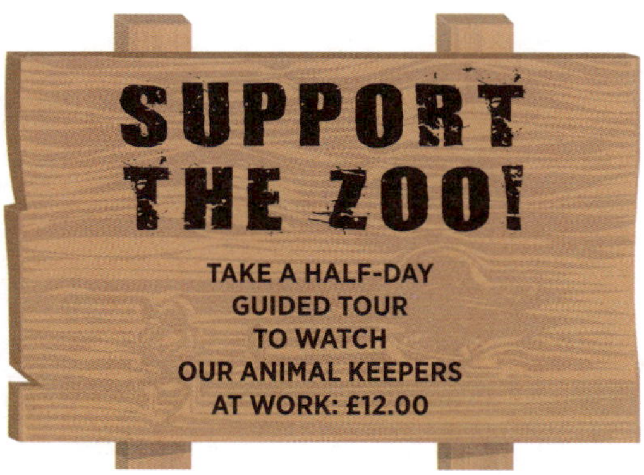

A5. Which of the following statements is correct?

A. ☐ Find out what our animal keepers do by taking our free half-day tour.

B. ☐ Visitors to the zoo today can try the work of the animal keepers.

C. ☐ By paying to spend some time with our animal keepers, you can help the zoo.

Part 2 | Questions A6 – A10

Leggi con attenzione le seguenti definizioni di alcuni termini. Qual è il termine corrispondente a ciascuna definizione? Associa le definizioni **A6 – A10** *con i termini* **A – G**. *Ci sono due termini extra, che non avrai bisogno di utilizzare.*

A6. ☐ It's a piece of furniture for keeping clothes.

A7. ☐ A man or a woman who instructs as a profession.

A8. ☐ It's an opening in the wall of a building or the side of a vehicle.

A9. ☐ They are white, in a row and are used to chew food.

A10. ☐ A large mammal with a long trunk and ivory tusks.

A. Teeth.

B. Wardrobe.

C. Window.

D. Flowers

E. Elephant.

F. Picture.

G. Teacher.

Part 3 | Questions A11 – A15

Leggi con attenzione le seguenti cinque brevi conversazioni. Per ciascuna di esse, scegli poi il completamento corretto (**A**, **B** *oppure* **C**) *in base a ciò che hai letto. Ti viene fornito un esempio* (**0**) *all'inizio.*

Example

0

A11. What are you doing this weekend?

A. ☐ I'm going to the concert.
B. ☐ I go to the concert.
C. ☐ I went to the concert.

A12. Where do you want to go shopping?

A. ☐ To the city centre.
B. ☐ I'd love to go to the circus.
C. ☐ No, I don't.

A13. What are you holding in your hand?

A. ☐ Give me five!
B. ☐ I think tomorrow.
C. ☐ My blue pen.

A14. How does the washing machine work?

A. ☐ Too much.
B. ☐ Not often.
C. ☐ Like this.

A15. How long did your exam last?

A. ☐ Yes, it's my last exam.
B. ☐ It lasted three hours.
C. ☐ It lasts three hours.

Part 4 | Questions A16 – A25

Leggi con attenzione il brano seguente e le relative domande. Per ciascun quesito, scegli poi la risposta corretta (**A**, **B**, **C** *oppure* **D**) *in base a ciò che hai letto.*

COCONUT ISLAND

When you think about the perfect holiday, the first image which comes to mind is that of white sand shores with a light blue sea and you are lying in the sun, drinking a cocktail or building sandcastles under the **palm trees**. Coconut Island is the ultimate beautiful, tropical island, rich with coconut palms, golden beaches and a clear blue sea. Well, it would be more accurate to say that Coconut Island was a wonderful island. Sunbeds, deckchairs and beach umbrellas used by hundreds of people have ruined the peaceful atmosphere of the past.

There are fewer coconut palm trees than before because they have been replaced by many tall buildings, hotels, holiday resorts, guest houses, restaurants, swimming pools now. You can still find golden beaches and clear blue sea, but the sea is full of **speedboats**, noisy jets skis and surfers. The natural paradise is lost, but Paradise Hotel is the best thing the island can offer. All the tourists are happy to spend their holidays on this tropical island: the weather is wonderful, not too hot and quite windy, the food is **tasty** and you don't have to pay a fortune at the restaurant, and the sea is warm all year round.

The local people seem happy too: they have the possibility to sell their local handcrafts (pottery, clothes, jewellery) on the beach, many people work in the resorts, as tour guides, receptionists, drivers or in local restaurants and gift shops.

Maybe it was so in the past but things have changed!
A friend of mine decided to go there seven years ago. She had a photo album full of wonderful pictures of deserted beaches of soft sand, with small, wooden bungalows in the middle of the sea. It was not necessary to book a hotel in advance and she had only to fly there and enjoy the quiet, peaceful island. The beach is always crowded with screaming people! There is music from the cafés, shouting children, and the hotels are very expensive. Most holidaymakers book their all-inclusive holidays even months before through the travel agencies.

Probably this may be called progress? The roads look better and there is also a new medical clinic. The local children can speak English and many new businesses are open all the time. The worst aspect of this apparently sparkling island is safety. When an old woman tries to cross the road from her house to the shops, she must be very careful and pay attention. Kids **race** around the island on motorbikes or quads and they don't ride bicycles anymore. And what about your **belongings**? If you decide to stay in a bungalow on the beach that had no lock, it's a good idea to put things in the safe box.
I don't know what the world's coming to!

GLOSSARY

palm trees (n) palme
speedboats (n) motoscafi
tasty (a) saporito
to race (v) gareggiare, sfidarsi
belongings (n) averi, effetti personali

A16. According to the text:

A. ☐ Coconut Island does not exist any longer.
B. ☐ Coconut Island is a beautiful, tropical island.
C. ☐ Coconut Island has always been full of people, sunbeds and umbrellas.
D. ☐ Coconut Island is not as beautiful as it was in the past.

A17. The term "speedboat" (line 9) means:

A. ☐ motorboat.
B. ☐ cabin.
C. ☐ jet.
D. ☐ motorbike.

A18. According to the text, all of the following are present in Coconut Island but:

A. ☐ clear blue sea.
B. ☐ coconut palms.
C. ☐ hotels.
D. ☐ pineapple trees.

A19. The writer:

A. ☐ is enjoying a holiday on Coconut Island.
B. ☐ might be the only person annoyed by the new features of Coconut Island.
C. ☐ appreciates all of the new comforts Coconut Island offers.
D. ☐ thinks that nothing on Coconut Island has changed at all.

A20. Are the following statements **true** or **false**? Tick as appropriate.

		True	False
a	Tourists on holiday on Coconut Island seem happy.		
b	Eating on Coconut Island is not as cheap as it should be.		
c	The weather on Coconut Island is not always good.		

A21. The reason why developers are certainly happy is that, on Coconut Island, there are a large number of:

....

A22. The author's friend:

A. ☐ went to Coconut Island once in her life.
B. ☐ decided to stop going to Coconut Island.
C. ☐ has a photo album full of pictures of Coconut Island.
D. ☐ said that booking a holiday to Coconut Island has always been important.

A23. Today:

A. ☐ Coconut Island's beaches are usually empty.
B. ☐ nothing is as beautiful as it was in the past on Coconut Island.
C. ☐ hotels on Coconut Island are at affordable prices.
D. ☐ his room is in Paradise Hotel.

A24. In the last paragraph the author:

A. ☐ complains about the noise coming from the children on the beach.
B. ☐ complains about the overcrowded beaches.
C. ☐ states that the island is not as safe as it was in the past.
D. ☐ complains about the absence of new medical clinics.

A25. The text above is, most probably:

A. ☐ an extract from a novel.
B. ☐ a review.
C. ☐ a proposal.
D. ☐ an article.

Part 5 | Questions A26 – A35

Leggi con attenzione il brano seguente sugli School Clubs. Indica poi se le affermazioni **A26** – **A35** *sono vere 'True'* (**A**), *false 'False'* (**B**) *o non menzionate dal testo 'Doesn't say'* (**C**).

What to do after school...

Most schools around the UK have after-school clubs which **are run** by teachers. There are sports clubs, music clubs, art clubs and even cookery clubs, all intended to improve children's education. So let's have a look at one school in Birmingham in central England and the after-school clubs they have on offer.

One of the most popular after-school clubs at the school is the Art Club. Students can do painting and **pottery** and even receive **tuition** from local artists. Every year, the club goes on a trip. Last year the club visited museums and art galleries in London, but this year the club is planning a trip to the Louvre Museum in Paris.

If you're not very good at Art, then how about volleyball? The school also has a superb Volleyball Club. When the weather is fine, students train outdoors on the volleyball courts but when it rains they play in the school gym. Every month, the team plays in a different **tournament** and wins lots of cups and awards.

Then there's the Chess Club if you don't like sport. The Chess Club has been active for three years now and students meet in the school library twice a week – on Mondays and Thursdays. Chess is a game which helps improve memory, problem-solving skills, and gives players an **enhanced** ability to think ahead. Chess expert Ivan Lenovic is giving a master-class one evening next term and the Chess Club is very excited!

The school also offers a healthy Cookery Club. This club started last year and was the idea of Mrs Jackson, the Science teacher. She told us that she thought the club was a great way to teach the importance of a healthy and balanced diet. It also teaches students how to plan and prepare meals, how to know what food is in season, and how to read and understand food labels. Students work in small groups of 6-7 children and have access to a refrigerator and oven.

As in many schools, there is also a performing Arts Club, which offers sessions of singing, dance and drama. Students meet three times a week after school in the drama theatre, and they work towards a show for parents at the end of each term. Students take part in theatre and drama games, and the club encourages students of all ages and talents. The drama teacher, Ms Holly, is passionate about inspiring and motivating children to take part in these activities because they help develop self-confidence and independence, as well as a love of performing.

GLOSSARY

to be run (v) essere gestiti
pottery (n) ceramica
tuition (n) lezione
tournament (n) torneo
to enhance (v) arricchire, migliorare

A26. Most UK schools have Science clubs.
A. ☐ true **B.** ☐ false **C.** ☐ doesn't say

A27. The Art Club visited the Louvre Museum in Paris last year.
A. ☐ true **B.** ☐ false **C.** ☐ doesn't say

A28. The school in Birmingham has a Volleyball Club.
A. ☐ true **B.** ☐ false **C.** ☐ doesn't say

A29. The volleyball courts are bigger than the gym.
A. ☐ true **B.** ☐ false **C.** ☐ doesn't say

A30. The Chess Club started last year.
A. ☐ true **B.** ☐ false **C.** ☐ doesn't say

A31. The Chess Club is only for students who can already play chess.
A. ☐ true **B.** ☐ false **C.** ☐ doesn't say

A32. Students need to bring an apron and kitchen utensils with them to the Cookery Club.
A. ☐ true **B.** ☐ false **C.** ☐ doesn't say

A33. The Cookery Club teaches children about fruit and vegetables in season.
A. ☐ true **B.** ☐ false **C.** ☐ doesn't say

A34. The Drama Club will not perform a show for the students' families.
A. ☐ true **B.** ☐ false **C.** ☐ doesn't say

A35. Ms Holly usually asks families to help with the costumes.
A. ☐ true **B.** ☐ false **C.** ☐ doesn't say

Section 2 – USE OF ENGLISH

Part 1 | Questions B1 – B5

*Leggi con attenzione il brano seguente su una gita a un parco giochi. Per ciascuno spazio, scegli poi il giusto completamento (**A**, **B** oppure **C**) in base a ciò che hai letto. Ti viene fornito un esempio (**0**) all'inizio del testo.*

Example

0	**A.** ☐ with	**B.** ☒ through	**C.** ☐ on

Where dreams come true

If you have never visited a theme park with your children, then expect to be amazed! We're talking about the magical little ways the parks will look different when you can see them (**0**) .... the eyes of a child. Disney's rich details cover every surface of the park.

Many of the most interesting and enchanting details in the Disney parks are around the eye level of (**B1**) .... smallest guests, while others are directly beneath your feet, where children are more likely **to spot** them on the ground.
If your children have their eyes **glued to the ground**, give them time. Instead, get down to their level to see what they're (**B2**) .... at. The streets around The Flying Carpets of Aladdin in Magic Kingdom have gems and coins in them. Planets and moons are featured in the pavement around Mission Space in Epcot.

Walt Disney Parks and Resorts give millions of guests each year the chance (**B3**) .... spend time with their families and friends, making memories that last a lifetime.
Disney offers something to look at no matter where your eye level falls. Disney's famous characters take on a whole new life when you have children (**B4**) .... you.

Disney's characters are trained to speak to children. Even the largest characters will do all they can to get down to the child's eye level and offer a gentle **high-five** or warm hug. One (**B5**) .... the most magical experiences you can have is watching a child rush to greet their favourite princess, fully believing that they're in the presence of real royalty.

GLOSSARY

to spot (v) individuare, riconoscere
glued to the ground incollati al suolo
high-five gesto 'dammi cinque'

B1.	**A.** ☐ its	**B.** ☐ her	**C.** ☐ our
B2.	**A.** ☐ watching	**B.** ☐ looking	**C.** ☐ flying
B3.	**A.** ☐ for	**B.** ☐ to	**C.** ☐ through
B4.	**A.** ☐ at	**B.** ☐ along	**C.** ☐ with
B5.	**A.** ☐ in	**B.** ☐ of	**C.** ☐ on

Part 2 | Questions B6 – B15

*Leggi con attenzione il brano seguente, poi scrivi la parola mancante in ciascuno spazio. Scrivi solo UNA parola per ciascuno spazio. Ti viene fornito un esempio (**0**) all'inizio del testo.*

Animals in the city

Recently, there were many reports (**0**) …in… newspapers and on TV about big animals coming (**B6**) .... towns and cities. There have been bears in Vancouver parks, leopards (**B7**) .... the streets of Mumbai and wild pigs in gardens in Berlin. What happens (**B8**) .... big animals come into our cities? Is it a good thing or is it dangerous (**B9**) .... us and the animals?

Wild animals usually come into cities (**B10**) .... look for food. In Cape Town, South Africa, baboons sometimes come into the suburbs. They eat fruit (**B11**) .... gardens and go into people's kitchens to find food. Baboons are big animals and sometimes they scare children and fight (**B12**) .... pet dogs. Many people do not like (**B13**) ...., but the city can be risky for baboons; sometimes, for example, baboons are hurt in car accidents.

The city council in Cape Town has a team (**B14**) .... Baboon Monitors. The Monitors have to find baboons in the city and take them (**B15**) .... to the savanna. This makes the city safer for people and it is healthier for the baboons. The problem is that a lot of baboons will come back to the city to find food again.

Section 3 – GRAMMAR KNOWLEDGE

Questions C1 – C10

Leggi con attenzione e rispondi ai seguenti quesiti di riflessione sulla lingua inglese.

C1. Complete the following sentence with the correct form of the verbs in brackets: present perfect or past simple?

Sarah is angry with Leonard. He ____________ (*to fail*) the Biology exam again and he also ____________ (*to fail*) the History exam last month.

C2. Complete the space in the following sentence appropriately: 'Mr Bianco is a ________ charming man'.

A. ☐ very much
B. ☐ lot
C. ☐ very
D. ☐ too

C3. Complete the following sentences, by deleting the wrong option appropriately.

a) Don't worry. I *won't forget/am not forgetting* to buy some bread on my way back home.
b) It's freezing today! It *will/is going to* snow later.
c) Do they know what *is happening/will happen* to that music contest in the future?

C4. Complete the space in the following sentence appropriately: 'Mark, there's a blue pen on the desk __________ to the television; can you pass it to me, please?'

A. ☐ next
B. ☐ beside
C. ☐ after
D. ☐ before

C5. Complete the space in the following sentence appropriately: 'If you finish work early, ________________ and see me at home.'

A. ☐ come around
B. ☐ come on
C. ☐ pass through
D. ☐ take off

C6. Complete the space in the following sentence appropriately: 'Her beloved cat's died suddenly, but Margaret will ____________ it in time.'

A. ☐ go on
B. ☐ get over
C. ☐ give up
D. ☐ be against

C7. Complete the space in the following sentence appropriately: 'Sasha always __________ her bed before going to school.'

A. ☐ makes
B. ☐ does
C. ☐ made
D. ☐ none of the other answers provided is correct

C8. Complete the space in the following sentence appropriately: 'Lisa, can you go __________ and fetch me a sweater? I'm a bit cold.'

A. ☐ along
B. ☐ through
C. ☐ towards
D. ☐ upstairs

C9. Complete the space in the following sentence appropriately: 'Paul doesn't watch tv. He doesn't read magazines __________.'

A. ☐ too
B. ☐ either
C. ☐ neither
D. ☐ never

C10. Complete the space in the following sentence appropriately: 'Bill reads a book for about three hours _________________ .'

A. ☐ every evening
B. ☐ all evening
C. ☐ every evenings
D. ☐ all evenings

Section 1 - Reading Skills	Section 2 - Use of English	Section 3 - Grammar Knowledge
Part 1 score .../5 Part 2 score .../5 Part 3 score .../5 Part 4 score .../10 Part 5 score .../10	Part 1 score .../5 Part 2 score .../10	Score .../10 **Total .../60**

Ho trovato la prova: ☐ Difficile ☐ Più semplice di quanto pensassi ☐ Adeguata alle mie aspettative e capacità ☐ Altro

Section 1 – READING SKILLS

Part 1 | Questions A1 – A5

Leggi con attenzione i seguenti brevi messaggi. Cosa dicono? Per ciascun quesito, scegli la risposta corretta (**A**, **B** oppure **C**) *in base a ciò che hai letto. Ti viene fornito un esempio* (**0**) *all'inizio.*

Example

0

Passengers:

A. ☐ must remember their own luggage when they leave.

B. ☒ must stay with their own luggage at all times.

C. ☐ cannot let someone else look after their luggage.

A1. Which of the following statements is correct?

A. ☐ You can take dogs to this apartment.

B. ☐ This flat is for those who are looking for something under £160,000.

C. ☐ You can park your car safely.

A2. The headmaster:

A. ☐ confirmed that piano lessons will take place as normal this week.

B. ☐ said that the new piano teacher can't start until next week.

C. ☐ said that piano lessons will begin again next week if they find a new piano teacher.

A3. According to the notice:

A. ☐ players can go into the changing rooms half an hour before the match begins.

B. ☐ only players from California High School can use these changing rooms.

C. ☐ the time of the game against California High School changed.

A4. The notice:

A. ☐ says that children can play with dogs only in this area.

B. ☐ says that you can't take your dog into this area.

C. ☐ refers to a new playground.

A5. Which of the following statements is correct?

A. ☐ You can make a lot of videos in this area.

B. ☐ Everything you do in this area is recorded.

C. ☐ You can record short videos.

Part 2 | Questions A6 – A10

Leggi con attenzione le seguenti definizioni di alcuni termini. Qual è il termine corrispondente a ciascuna definizione? Associa le definizioni **A6 – A10** *con i termini* **A – G**. *Ci sono due termini extra, che non avrai bisogno di utilizzare.*

A6. ☐ A road vehicle, typically with four wheels, which can carry a small number of people.

A7. ☐ It is a thin instrument for writing or drawing.

A8. ☐ It is a short, narrow board with two small wheels fixed to the bottom of either end.

A9. ☐ A man whose job is to serve customers at their tables in a restaurant.

A10. ☐ A telephone which can be used over a wide area, without physical connection to a network.

A. Skateboard.

B. Mobile phone.

C. Waiter.

D. Song.

E. Pencil.

F. Cotton.

G. Car.

Part 3 | Questions A11 – A15

Leggi con attenzione le seguenti cinque brevi conversazioni. Per ciascuna di esse, scegli poi il completamento corretto (**A**, **B** *oppure* **C**) *in base a ciò che hai letto. Ti viene fornito un esempio* (**0**) *all'inizio.*

Example

0

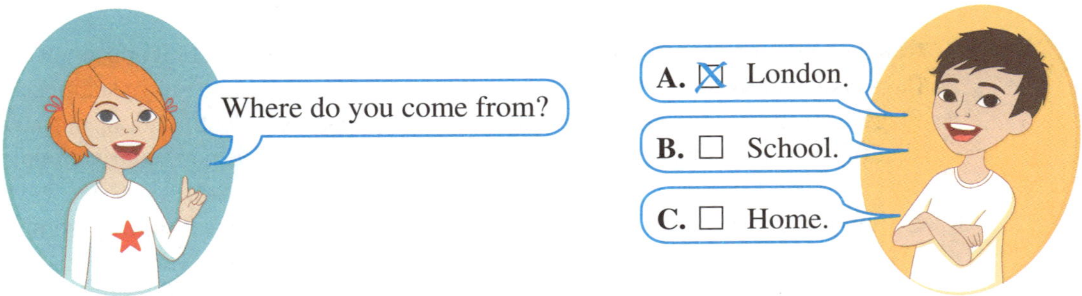

A11. Is there any orange juice in the fridge?

A. ☐ No, it is not.
B. ☐ Have a look!
C. ☐ They prefer salads.

A12. Do you have any brothers or sisters?

A. ☐ At least ten.
B. ☐ I have two sisters.
C. ☐ No, they don't.

A13. Whose is that jacket?

A. ☐ I think it's blue!
B. ☐ That jacket is large.
C. ☐ It's Paul's.

A14. Where are your black shoes?

A. ☐ Under the chair.
B. ☐ In the desk.
C. ☐ Behind the wall.

A15. What do you want to be when you grow up?

A. ☐ I saw a policeman.
B. ☐ A policeman.
C. ☐ I was a policeman.

Part 4 | Questions A16 – A25

*Leggi con attenzione il brano seguente e le relative domande. Per ciascun quesito, scegli poi la risposta corretta (**A**, **B**, **C** oppure **D**) in base a ciò che hai letto.*

WAVING FLAGS

Can we really represent an entire nation on a piece of **cloth**? Well, it appears we can. National flags can be seen everywhere from **courthouses** and classrooms to fire stations and museums. Flags were originally used on battlefields as a **means** of identification, but now have great significance to nations around the world and their designs have particularly complex meanings.

During the 2006 World Cup, the English flag could be seen **hanging** from car windows, from the top of houses and in the street. English flags were everywhere – in fact, during this period England was just a sea of red and white! Before 1996, however, English people often waved the British flag during football matches, but during the 1996 European Football Championship England played against Scotland and no English football **supporter** wanted to **wave** the 'Union Jack' (the national flag of the United Kingdom) quite simply because it includes the Scottish flag.

So what do we know about other flags that were flying during the 2006 World Cup? Well, there's the Australian flag, for example, which also includes the Union Jack. Then, there were the only two flags with writing on them, those of Brazil and Saudi Arabia.

The Brazilian flag is written in Portuguese while the Saudi Arabian flag has religious words written in Arabic. Being written in Arabic means that the **flagpole** is on the left of the flag so that the writing can be read from left to right. Another flag flying during the World Cup in 2006 was that of Switzerland, which consists of a red square with a red cross in the centre. While symbols for the ICRC (International Committee of the Red Cross) include a red cross on a white background (a reversal of the Swiss flag), a red **crescent** and, since 2005, also a red crystal.

One tricolour flag flying at the 2006 World Cup, however, will never be seen again because just before the competition Serbia and Montenegro became independent states, and as a consequence, their football team represented a country that simply no longer existed.

And finally, there's the flag of Paraguay, which although in the common red, white and blue colours, it is also unique in that it has two different sides to it. One side shows the national **coat of arms** while the other has a different **emblem**. So, as you can see, flags are not all they appear to be… they can be a colourful, interesting, unusual and unique way of identifying a country.

GLOSSARY

cloth (n) tessuto
courthouse (n) palazzo di giustizia
means (n) mezzo, strumento
to hang (v) appendere
supporter (n) tifoso
to wave (v) sventolare
flagpole (n) asta portabandiera
crescent (n) mezzaluna
coat of arms (n) insegna
emblem (n) emblema, simbolo

A16. During the World Cup in 2006:

A. ☐ many English people started to fly the English flag.
B. ☐ everybody was happy to fly the British flag.
C. ☐ everybody was happy to fly the English flag.
D. ☐ many English people started to fly the British flag.

A17. Before 1996:

A. ☐ England played against Scotland.
B. ☐ England was a sea of red and white.
C. ☐ the Union Jack was flying at the World Cup.
D. ☐ people didn't use to fly the English flag.

A18. Other flags that were flying in the World Cup in 2006 included Saudi Arabia's that had writing on it in:

....

A19. The Saudi Arabian flag:

A. ☐ didn't fly in the World Cup in 2006.
B. ☐ has religious words on it.
C. ☐ has been used on T-shirts.
D. ☐ has a flagpole on the right.

A20. The Swiss flag:

A. ☐ didn't fly in the World Cup in 2006.
B. ☐ includes a flower.
C. ☐ is square.
D. ☐ includes a white cross on a red background.

A21. The oldest tricolour is the:

A. ☐ Italian flag.
B. ☐ Netherlands flag.
C. ☐ French flag.
D. ☐ The information is not present in the text.

A22. Are the following statements **true** or **false**? Tick as appropriate.

		True	False
a	The Swiss flag isn't a tricolour.		
b	The Serbian and Montenegro flag used to be the same.		
c	The Australian flag includes the Union Jack.		

A23. During the World Cup in 2006:

A. ☐ there were ten countries taking part in the competition.
B. ☐ there was a flag that can no longer be seen.
C. ☐ Costa Rica's flag was not flying.
D. ☐ none of the answers provided is correct.

A24. According to the text:

A. ☐ Paraguay's flag is one-sided.
B. ☐ Serbia and Montenegro decided to become independent states before the World Cup in 2006.
C. ☐ the Brazilian flag isn't written in Portuguese.
D. ☐ two square national flags were flying in the World Cup in 2006.

A25. The text above is, most probably:

A. ☐ an extract from a novel.
B. ☐ a review.
C. ☐ a proposal.
D. ☐ an article from a journal.

Part 5 | Questions A26 – A35

Leggi con attenzione il brano seguente sulle mete preferite per le vacanze. Indica poi se le affermazioni **A26** – **A35** *sono vere 'True'* (**A**), *false 'False'* (**B**) *o non menzionate dal testo 'Doesn't say'* (**C**).

The ideal holiday destinations!

Popular destinations	People holiday with...
A city break 22%	Partner only 31%
A beach holiday 47%	Close relatives 50%
All-inclusive holiday 17%	Extended family 15%
A cruise 14%	Alone 4%

A holiday destination may be the best location for one person but not for another. It all depends on what you mean by ideal holiday, a sightseeing tour in the most important world capitals, or lazily lying in the sun drinking a cocktail, or experiencing amazing adventures in less touristic location.

Some places in the world are so incredible that it is almost impossible not to love them. Just think about the millions of people who keep on queing at Madame Tussauds museum to enjoy the **wax** statues of the singers or actors they love.

You can check the degree of popularity of a holiday destination in a number of different ways: internet searches, research **polls** or booking data.

Even though, **whichever way you cut it**, Mallorca consistently tops all lists for travellers as the most popular holiday destination, thanks to its great beaches, beautiful mountains and various activities suitable for families, couples and even singles. If you want a holiday full of fun and sun, but you can't stand long flights, Mallorca offers the perfect mixture of relaxation and island escape with a flight time of just over 2 hours.

Another favourite holiday destination for young people is the party capital of Europe, Ibiza, which offers fantastic nightlife and lots of opportunities for visitors to enjoy its charming whitewashed villages, sandy coves and pretty pine forests, as well as its legendary club scene. Now, the above information might make it sound like a nightmare for some but Ibiza isn't just a party destination, and it can be enjoyed by families or groups of friends who don't want to spend all night, every night, in a club.

Most of those who choose Orlando as their holiday destination, go there to explore theme parks and to seek fun and sun. However, tourists need to know that there is much more to explore in Orlando, besides the world famous Walt Disney, Universal Studios and Harry Potter theme parks. They can also visit interesting museums, beautiful parks, local restaurants and fashion shops, enjoy entertaining shows, pools, water parks, the Kennedy Space Center, Daytona Beach and much, much more! In fact, Orlando represents the most popular destination for British tourists!

GLOSSARY

wax (n) cera
polls (n) sondaggi
whichever way you cut it (v) in qualunque modo la giri

A26. It is most common for people to go on holiday with their partner.
A. ☐ true **B.** ☐ false **C.** ☐ doesn't say

A27. More that 2 million people visit Madame Tussauds every year.
A. ☐ true **B.** ☐ false **C.** ☐ doesn't say

A28. City breaks continue to maintain their leading position as the favourite holiday type.
A. ☐ true **B.** ☐ false **C.** ☐ doesn't say

A29. Mallorca can be very expensive for tourists.
A. ☐ true **B.** ☐ false **C.** ☐ doesn't say

A30. Florida is a very popular destination for tourists from the UK.
A. ☐ true **B.** ☐ false **C.** ☐ doesn't say

A31. Most people prefer to go on holiday with their partners and children in winter.
A. ☐ true **B.** ☐ false **C.** ☐ doesn't say

A32. 4% of people prefer to travel on their own.
A. ☐ true **B.** ☐ false **C.** ☐ doesn't say

A33. A tourist finds nothing to do in Ibiza.
A. ☐ true **B.** ☐ false **C.** ☐ doesn't say

A34. You can know how popular a holiday destination is via the internet.
A. ☐ true **B.** ☐ false **C.** ☐ doesn't say

A35. Daytona Beach is in Ibiza.
A. ☐ true **B.** ☐ false **C.** ☐ doesn't say

Section 2 – USE OF ENGLISH

Part 1 | Questions B1 – B5

Leggi con attenzione il brano seguente sull'Australia. Per ciascuno spazio, scegli poi il giusto completamento (**A**, **B** *oppure* **C**) *in base a ciò che hai letto. Ti viene fornito un esempio* (**0**) *all'inizio del testo.*

Example

0	**A.** ☒ an	**B.** ☐ on	**C.** ☐ off

DOWN UNDER

Australia is the only country in the world that covers (**0**) .... entire continent, but surprisingly it is the largest island in the world as well! More than 24 million people (**B1**) .... in Australia, which are not so many if you consider how big this country is. The majority of the country is desert, which is called the *outback*.

The capital is Canberra but its largest urban area is Sydney. Another important city is Alice Springs, which is collocated in the (**B2**) .... of the *outback*. Tourists come to Alice Springs because they can try different adventure sports in the desert, like camping, mountain biking and walking. You can't miss the experience of flying (**B3**) .... the desert in a hot air balloon, a helicopter or a small plane. The first explorers crossed the *outback* using camels.

The first people to live in Australia were the Aborigines, and they've (**B4**) .... there for approximately 50,000 years! Today the Aborigines live in the desert areas of the Australian *outback* and they've learnt to survive under these harsh desert conditions.

Australia was first called New Holland because it was discovered by Dutch explorers. Australia's nickname is *Down Under* as it is faraway, but also because it has got unique animals and plants that can't be found anywhere else in the world, such as kangaroos, echidnas, kookaburras and koalas.

The Great Barrier Reef is the biggest (**B5**) .... reef in the world. It is made up of more than 3,000 reefs, and there are more than 1,500 species of fish!

The Australian flag has three parts, the Commonwealth Star, the Southern Cross and the Union Jack. Australia is a member of the Commonwealth of Nations, and this means that the head of state is Queen Elizabeth II!

B1.	**A.** ☐ alive	**B.** ☐ live	**C.** ☐ life
B2.	**A.** ☐ middle	**B.** ☐ half	**C.** ☐ between
B3.	**A.** ☐ under	**B.** ☐ in	**C.** ☐ over
B4.	**A.** ☐ been	**B.** ☐ gone	**C.** ☐ were
B5.	**A.** ☐ local	**B.** ☐ coral	**C.** ☐ choral

Part 2 | Questions B6 – B15

Leggi con attenzione il brano seguente, poi scrivi la parola mancante in ciascuno spazio. Scrivi solo UNA parola per ciascuno spazio. Ti viene fornito un esempio (**0**) *all'inizio del testo.*

THE ART OF GRAFFITI

In the 1970s, some young people (**0**) ..... in ..... New York used ordinary pens to write their names on the big city walls. One (**B6**) .... the first taggers was called Pablo, a teenager (**B7**) .... a Mexican family. Most people say that Pablo was not his real name. He loved to sign his works with the tag PfM 2507, where PfM was (**B8**) .... nickname and meant Pablo from Mexico (as he was proud of his origins) and 2507 was the number of the house (**B9**) .... he lived – 2507 Madison Street. His first tags were left on his neighbours' walls when he was only twelve and they were not very happy to see those labels on their building, as they considered them an act of vandalism. Later he started writing his trademark in subway stations when he travelled to school. When the train stopped at a station, he jumped (**B10**) ...., wrote his marker on the wall and then jumped back on the train before the doors closed. Pablo inspired other teenagers who began writing (**B11**) .... personal tags everywhere on benches, fountains, walls, buses and trains all over New York.

At a certain point some taggers changed their pens with aerosol paints, so their graffiti became bigger and (**B12**) .... colourful. Then, in (**B13**) .... 1970s and 1980s, aerosol paint graffiti started to become very popular all around the world and appeared for the first time on walls, trains and buses. In the 2000s, a lot of graffiti artists started to create beautiful pictures which represented their inner feelings or beliefs. Some artists were interested in politics and tried (**B14**) .... use their pieces of art to make people think about social problems and discrimination (**B15**) .... their pictures. On the other hand, for some artists the only aim of their art was making cities more attractive. In South America, street artists brought colour and beauty to grey city walls.

Section 3 – GRAMMAR KNOWLEDGE

Questions C1 – C10

Leggi con attenzione e rispondi ai seguenti quesiti di riflessione sulla lingua inglese.

C1. Complete the following sentences, by deleting the wrong option appropriately.

a) There aren't *any/~~no~~* pictures on your sister's bedroom walls.
b) 'How much luggage have you got, Sarah?' *None/Any*
c) The weather was cold, but there was *no/none* wind.

C2. Complete the space in the following sentence appropriately: 'My new lamp doesn't work. I am going to ____________ to the shop.'

A. ☐ take it back
B. ☐ turn it on
C. ☐ bring it
D. ☐ pick it up

C3. Complete the space in the following sentence appropriately: 'Wait a minute, Jack! Don't go __________ because I want to ask you something.'

A. ☐ back
B. ☐ away
C. ☐ down
D. ☐ on

C4. Complete the space in the following sentence appropriately: 'Why are you so tired? Did you __________ to bed late last night?'

A. ☐ go
B. ☐ been
C. ☐ went
D. ☐ were

C5. Complete the space in the following sentence appropriately: '_______________. Can you close that window over there, please?'

A. ☐ It has cold
B. ☐ I'm cold
C. ☐ I cold
D. ☐ I have cold

C6. Complete the space in the following sentence appropriately: 'Tommy has been in Canada _________________ now.'

A. ☐ six months ago
B. ☐ for six months
C. ☐ since six months
D. ☐ in six months

C7. Complete the space in the following sentence appropriately: 'That hospital over there _________________ more than 100 years ago.'

A. ☐ is built
B. ☐ was built
C. ☐ built
D. ☐ was building

C8. Complete the space in the following sentence appropriately: 'It _________________, so we didn't need an umbrella.'

A. ☐ wasn't rain
B. ☐ wasn't raining
C. ☐ didn't raining
D. ☐ wasn't rained

C9. Complete the space in the following sentence appropriately: 'I am having a party on the 23rd of May, but Richard and Ingrid _______________ .'

A. ☐ can't come

B. ☐ couldn't come

C. ☐ can't coming

D. ☐ can't to come

C10. Which of the following sentences is incorrect?

A. ☐ Shall we meet us at 9 am?

B. ☐ Why don't we meet at 9 am?

C. ☐ Shall we meet up at 9 am?

D. ☐ How about meeting at 9 am?

Section 1 - Reading Skills	Section 2 - Use of English	Section 3 - Grammar Knowledge
Part 1 score .../5 Part 2 score .../5 Part 3 score .../5 Part 4 score .../10 Part 5 score .../10	Part 1 score .../5 Part 2 score .../10	Score .../10 **Total .../60**

Ho trovato la prova: ☐ Difficile ☐ Più semplice di quanto pensassi ☐ Adeguata alle mie aspettative e capacità ☐ Altro

Section 1 – READING SKILLS

Part 1 | Questions A1 – A5

Leggi con attenzione i seguenti brevi messaggi. Cosa dicono? Per ciascun quesito, scegli la risposta corretta (**A**, **B** oppure **C**) *in base a ciò che hai letto. Ti viene fornito un esempio* (**0**) *all'inizio.*

Example

0

Passengers:

A. ☐ must remember their own luggage when they leave.

B. ☒ must stay with their own luggage at all times.

C. ☐ cannot let someone else look after their luggage.

A1. The computers:

A. ☐ do not have Windows system installed.

B. ☐ do not have wi-fi connections.

C. ☐ will provide ample space for your personal files.

A2. The note says that:

A. ☐ you must clean your tennis shoes before playing.

B. ☐ proper tennis shoes can be rented from the club.

C. ☐ everyone must wear the correct shoes on these courts.

A3. Which of the following statements is correct?

A. ☐ The five-week course is cheaper if you also do the one-day class.

B. ☐ The one-day class is free for those who book the five-week course.

C. ☐ You must pay for the five-week course before you do the one-day class.

A4. The notice:

A. ☐ allows only dogs to enter.

B. ☐ clearly states that trained service animals are admitted.

C. ☐ reminds people to keep pets and animals under control.

A5. Which of the following statements is correct?

A. ☐ You don't need to pay to get the bus from here.

B. ☐ Booking the free bus service is not necessary.

C. ☐ If you ask the reception, you will have a discount.

Part 2 | Questions A6 – A10

Leggi con attenzione le seguenti definizioni di alcuni termini. Qual è il termine corrispondente a ciascuna definizione? Associa le definizioni **A6 – A10** *con i termini* **A – G**. *Ci sono due termini extra, che non avrai bisogno di utilizzare.*

A6. ☐ It's an instrument for measuring and recording time.

A7. ☐ A person who makes, builds or repairs wooden things.

A8. ☐ It's a herb or other small vegetable that grows in the earth.

A9. ☐ They are electroacoustic devices that are a component in an audio system.

A10. ☐ It's the star around which the planets revolve and from which they receive light and heat.

A. Plant.

B. Carpenter.

C. Dancer.

D. Painter.

E. Clock.

F. The Sun.

G. Speakers.

Part 3 | Questions A11 – A15

Leggi con attenzione le seguenti cinque brevi conversazioni. Per ciascuna di esse, scegli poi il completamento corretto (**A**, **B** *oppure* **C**) *in base a ciò che hai letto. Ti viene fornito un esempio* (**0**) *all'inizio.*

Example

0

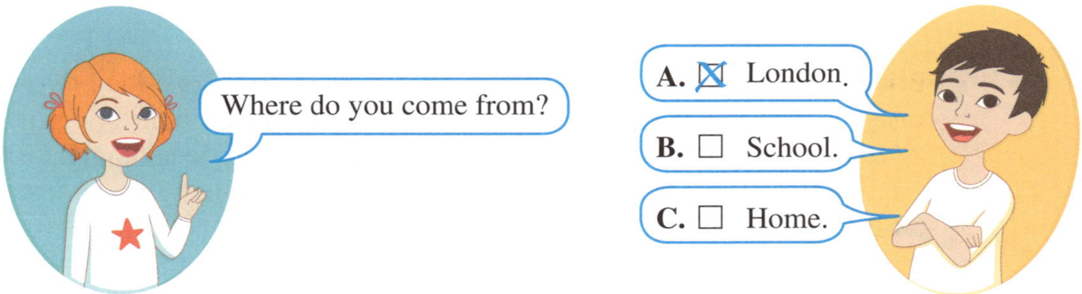

A11. What was the weather like when the holiday began?
- **A.** ☐ It's going to rain.
- **B.** ☐ It was cloudy.
- **C.** ☐ I feel cold.

A12. Who gave the man the CD for his birthday?
- **A.** ☐ In the best shop ever.
- **B.** ☐ I'll buy him a new DVD.
- **C.** ☐ It was his wife's idea.

A13. Which radio programme is about to begin?
- **A.** ☐ Time for cooking!
- **B.** ☐ I don't like sports so much.
- **C.** ☐ Turn it off, please!

A14. What computer game has the boy just bought?
- **A.** ☐ I prefer ball games.
- **B.** ☐ He never plays videogames.
- **C.** ☐ The latest war game.

A15. What does the woman plan to do in the mountains?
- **A.** ☐ She'd like to go skiing.
- **B.** ☐ She is able to climb mountains.
- **C.** ☐ Mountains are only for experts.

Part 4 | Questions A16 – A25

*Leggi con attenzione il brano seguente e le relative domande. Per ciascun quesito, scegli poi la risposta corretta (**A**, **B**, **C** oppure **D**) in base a ciò che hai letto.*

BRIDGES

Bridges are everywhere, aren't they? They're there to cross a long river, a **crowded** road or a railway line and can be a very exciting experience. If the bridge is particularly high, you may feel like you're flying. If the bridge is very long, it might take you ages to get to the other side. If the bridge is very narrow, you may even be scared of falling off the side!

There are some amazing bridges to **cross** around the world. In the USA, there's the Golden Gate Bridge in San Francisco, in Australia there's the Sydney Harbour Bridge, in Zimbabwe you can cross the Zambezi river to Zambia, while there's the medieval Ponte Vecchio bridge in Florence and in Thailand the Friendship Bridge to Laos. Then of course there's London where there are so many bridges. In fact, there are about 214 bridges across the river Thames and 34 of these are in the capital itself. So, the announcement that a new bridge was to be built to celebrate the Millennium was no surprise for many Londoners.

It was to be the first new pedestrian bridge for 100 years with no cars, trains or pollution – just people! Running from St. Paul's Cathedral to Southwark, 320 metres long and 4 metres wide, the Millennium Bridge was opened in June 2000. There was great excitement when the bridge opened. So much so that 100,000 people crossed the bridge in the first weekend. In his opening speech, the mayor of London, Ken Livingstone, said: 'It will be so good to actually walk across the river peacefully, without cars and trains thundering by.' It was a very exciting experience for many, walking slowly across the bridge and looking down at the river 11 metres below.

Unfortunately, however, the bridge moved just a little too much. In fact, it moved to the left and then it moved to the right – it was literally swinging! This lateral movement caused a great deal of alarm and many people were then too scared to cross the bridge. Two days after its opening, the bridge was promptly closed and it had a new name too: not the Millennium Bridge but the **Wobbly** Bridge (not officially of course!). Although the architect said there wasn't a problem and that the bridge was **designed** to move, it was only reopened 20 months later after substantial modifications were made to eliminate the swaying.

GLOSSARY

crowded (a) affollato
to cross (v) attraversare
wobbly (a) barcollante
to design (v) progettare

A16. The author of the text:

A. ☐ thinks high bridges are very scary.
B. ☐ hates walking across bridges.
C. ☐ suggests you may be afraid on a narrow bridge.
D. ☐ doesn't like bridges at all.

A17. Zambezi:

A. ☐ is the name of a town in Zimbabwe.
B. ☐ is the name of a river in Zimbabwe.
C. ☐ is the name of a bridge in Zimbabwe.
D. ☐ is the other name of Zambia.

A18. The Golden Gate is the name of an American:

....

A19. In London:

A. ☐ there are exactly 37 bridges.
B. ☐ there are 214 bridges.
C. ☐ there is a large number of bridges.
D. ☐ there are only 30 bridges across the Thames.

A20. The term 'pedestrian' (line 14) means:

A. ☐ suburban.
B. ☐ metropolitan.
C. ☐ urban.
D. ☐ walker.

A21. The Millennium Bridge:

A. ☐ is near Chelsea Bridge.
B. ☐ arrives at St Paul's Cathedral.
C. ☐ is accessible to trains and cars.
D. ☐ is 320 m long and 4 m wide.

A22. During a sunny Saturday in June 2000:

A. ☐ the Millennium Bridge closed.
B. ☐ the author was not so happy.
C. ☐ the author decided not to walk across the bridge.
D. ☐ the Millennium Bridge was inaugurated.

A23. While walking across the Millennium Bridge, many people felt the bridge:

....

A24. Are the following statements **true** or **false**? Tick as appropriate.

		True	False
a	While walking across the Millennium Bridge, pedestrians were very excited.		
b	While walking across the Millennium Bridge, the bridge was swinging.		
c	The Mayor of London wasn't very happy to see another bridge built in the city.		

A25. The Millennium Bridge:

A. ☐ hasn't reopened yet.
B. ☐ was closed on the same day it opened.
C. ☐ was officially renamed the Wobbly Bridge.
D. ☐ was reopened when engineers were sure it wouldn't sway anymore.

Part 5 | Questions A26 – A35

Leggi con attenzione il brano seguente sugli animali in pericolo di estinzione. Indica poi se le affermazioni **A26** – **A35** *sono vere 'True'* (**A**), *false 'False'* (**B**) *o non menzionate dal testo 'Doesn't say'* (**C**).

Wildlife in danger!

Endangered species		
Tiger	Africa/Asia	around 13,000 specimens
Blue whale	world's oceans	fewer than 25,000 specimens
Mountain gorilla	Africa	around 880 specimens
Giant panda	China	fewer than 2,500 specimens

There are estimated to be about 30 million animal species on the planet, a large number of which are in danger of extinction. These endangered species are **threatened** by many things, including habitat loss, **hunting**, disease and climate change, and usually, endangered species also have a declining population. The statistics are quite shocking if we think that current estimates suggest that a third of the world's amphibians, one in eight birds and a quarter of all mammals, are endangered.

Animals are a beautiful, amazing part of the natural world, and they are also of great global economic importance. They maintain the ecosystems essential to our existence by helping to regulate our climate and by providing clean water and air, food, building and clothing materials and fertile soils.

So, what kind of animals are in danger of extinction? Well, four subspecies of tiger living in parts of Asia - the Caspian, Javan, Balinese, and South China tigers - have already become extinct **due to** habitat loss and hunting by humans. Many are killed for their bones, eyes and skin. Only five subspecies remain: the Amur, or Siberian tiger, the Bengal tiger, the Indochinese tiger, the Malayan tiger, and the Sumatran tiger.

Then there is the **dwindling** number of whales around the world. Although found in all of the world's oceans apart from The Arctic, there are now fewer than 25,000 living blue whales, the largest animals on the planet. As a result of 20th century whaling, the current population has been reduced by up to 90%, despite the fact that commercial hunting of the species was ultimately banned in 1966. To help in the battle against extinction, The US National Marine Fisheries Service stipulated the maintenance of photo databases of individual specimens and the collection of genetic and migration data in order to better understand the species which remains at risk from ship collisions and **entanglement** in fishing nets.

Who, of course, can forget the black and white panda? Everyone loves a panda. Unfortunately, China, which is home to the remaining wild population, has fewer than 2,500 specimens. Since the late 1980s, however, the country has instituted more stringent habitat protections. Sadly, the pandas are still subject to disease, occasional predation, and **starvation** when large bamboo trees on which they feed complete their life cycle and die. In a constant battle to reduce panda extinction, in 2014, China outlawed the consumption of endangered species, whose organs are believed to have magical curative powers.

GLOSSARY

threatened (v) minacciate
hunting (n) caccia
due to a causa di
dwindling in diminuzione
entanglement (n) intrico, groviglio
starvation (n) fame

A26. Hunting does not represent a cause for animals' extinction.
A. ☐ true **B.** ☐ false **C.** ☐ doesn't say

A27. 33% of the world's amphibians and 25% of all mammals are endangered.
A. ☐ true **B.** ☐ false **C.** ☐ doesn't say

A28. Mountain gorillas are moving from Africa to Asia.
A. ☐ true **B.** ☐ false **C.** ☐ doesn't say

A29. There are more than 25,000 specimens of blue whale in the world's oceans.
A. ☐ true **B.** ☐ false **C.** ☐ doesn't say

A30. South China tigers are among the endangered species.
A. ☐ true **B.** ☐ false **C.** ☐ doesn't say

A31. Commercial hunting of blue whales has never been banned.
A. ☐ true **B.** ☐ false **C.** ☐ doesn't say

A32. Blue whales live in all of the world's oceans but not in the Arctic Ocean.
A. ☐ true **B.** ☐ false **C.** ☐ doesn't say

A33. The worst threats for blue whales are ship collisions and fishing nets.
A. ☐ true **B.** ☐ false **C.** ☐ doesn't say

A34. Bamboo is the main source of nutrition for the Giant Panda.
A. ☐ true **B.** ☐ false **C.** ☐ doesn't say

A35. In 2014 China decided to grow new bamboo trees to help the Giant Panda survive.
A. ☐ true **B.** ☐ false **C.** ☐ doesn't say

Section 2 – USE OF ENGLISH

Part 1 | Questions B1 – B5

*Leggi con attenzione il brano seguente sui fenicotteri. Per ciascuno spazio, scegli poi il giusto completamento (**A**, **B** oppure **C**) in base a ciò che hai letto. Ti viene fornito un esempio (**0**) all'inizio del testo.*

Example

0 **A.** ☐ blue **B.** ☐ green **C.** ☒ pink

FLAMINGOES' SECRETS

Have you ever seen the image of a pink bird standing isolated on white background? Flamingoes are popular all over the world for their bright (**0**) .... feathers, long thin legs, and S-shaped neck. Their favourite dinner includes fish, shrimp, snails, and algae and to get them, it **plunges** its head into the water, twists it upside down, and take the fish using its upper beak. They are able to run (**B1**) .... water, because they are **endowed with** webbed feet, to gain speed before lifting up into the sky.

Flamingoes build nests for only one egg. The female and the male take turns sitting on the (**B2**) .... to keep it warm for about 30 days until the egg **hatches**. Baby flamingoes have white, soft feathers. Both parents feed the newborn flamingo with a fluid produced in their digestive systems.

After five or six days the young flamingo leaves the nest to join other young specimen in small groups but they always return to the parents for food. After about twenty-two days, young flamingoes start to look for food on their own.

Have you ever wondered why flamingoes are able to sleep while standing on one (**B3**) .... ? Researchers in Atlanta, USA, say they can stand on just one leg for many hours because of their skeleton structure. The flamingo's **hips** and leg bones are in a special shape and position that give the (**B4**) .... balance. The position of the bones in a flamingo means the birds do not need to use so many muscles to **keep still**. Some French biologists suggest that standing on one leg may allow the birds to save energy and conserve more body heat, since they spend a lot of time splashing in cold water.

Another researcher, Dr Geoffrey Michigan, said that it would be very difficult for a human to stay still without (**B5**) ...., even for an hour. You could try, if you want to! A man's muscles constantly change to keep us straight and prevent us from falling over.

GLOSSARY

to plunge (v) tuffarsi, lanciarsi in qualcosa
endowed with (a) dotati di
to hatche (v) schiudersi
hips (n) fianchi, anche
to keep still (v) stare fermo

B1.	**A.** ☐ in	**B.** ☐ on	**C.** ☐ under
B2.	**A.** ☐ egg	**B.** ☐ male	**C.** ☐ water
B3.	**A.** ☐ hand	**B.** ☐ toe	**C.** ☐ leg
B4.	**A.** ☐ fish	**B.** ☐ bird	**C.** ☐ insect
B5.	**A.** ☐ moving	**B.** ☐ sleeping	**C.** ☐ flying

Part 2 | Questions B6 – B15

Leggi con attenzione il brano seguente, poi scrivi la parola mancante in ciascuno spazio. Scrivi solo UNA parola per ciascuno spazio. Ti viene fornito un esempio (**0**) *all'inizio del testo.*

A book review

In 2001, the Canadian author Yann Martel published a fiction book entitled *The Life of Pi*, that tells the story of a young teenage boy (**0**) ...from... India, whose name was Pi, who one day finds himself trapped (**B6**) .... a tiger on a boat in the Pacific Ocean. This novel, which is the third one (**B7**) .... the author Yann Martel, has sold about seven million copies all over the world, has won several prestigious prizes and has been translated (**B8**) .... more than forty different languages.

(**B9**) .... the start of the book, we read that Pi spent his childhood in Pondicherry, a small district in India. When Pi turns 16, his parents decide to close down their zoo and completely change their lives, moving to Canada. While they are sailing to Canada, the ship sinks because of a terrible storm. Unfortunately, all Pi's family members and the sailors die (**B10**) .... the storm, but Pi survives and finds himself in a boat with a hyena, a zebra, an orangutan and a huge tiger. One by one, the animals start to kill and eat (**B11**) .... other for survival, and in the end only Pi and the tiger stay alive. Luckily (**B12**) .... Pi, there is enough food and water to carry on, but soon the only way to get something to eat every day was catching fish. He also gave food to the tiger (**B13**) .... prevent it from killing and eating him because of hunger.

Pi and the tiger spend more than two hundred days together on the lifeboat. They are also able to get (**B14**) .... terrible storms and the burning heat of the Pacific sun. They are often hungry and ill. Sometimes, Pi feels sad and lonely, other times he finds comfort in his three religions, until they finally arrive at the coast of Mexico, but you will have to read the book to find (**B15**) .... what happens in the end!

Section 3 – GRAMMAR KNOWLEDGE

Questions C1 – C10

Leggi con attenzione e rispondi ai seguenti quesiti di riflessione sulla lingua inglese.

C1. Complete the space in the following sentence appropriately: 'When did Alice go out?' '________________________.'

A. ☐ For twenty minutes
B. ☐ Since twenty minutes
C. ☐ In twenty minutes
D. ☐ Twenty minutes ago

C2. Complete the space in the following sentence appropriately: '____________________ to the cinema on Sunday evening. Do you want to come with us?'

A. ☐ We go
B. ☐ We will go
C. ☐ We are going
D. ☐ We will going

C3. Complete the space in the following sentence appropriately: 'There's a good film on TV tonight. ________________________ it.'

A. ☐ I watch
B. ☐ I'll watch
C. ☐ I'm going to watch
D. ☐ I'll watching

C4. Complete the space in the following sentence appropriately: 'You haven't met my mother yet, ____________________?'

A. ☐ have you
B. ☐ did you
C. ☐ haven't you
D. ☐ do you

C5. Complete the space in the following sentence appropriately: 'Excuse me, ________________ a hotel near here?'

A. ☐ there is
B. ☐ is there
C. ☐ is it
D. ☐ has there

C6. Complete the space in the following sentence appropriately: 'When ______________________________?' 'I am not sure… More than 100 years ago.'

A. ☐ was the telephone invented
B. ☐ has the telephone invented
C. ☐ was invented the telephone
D. ☐ did the telephone invented

C7. Complete the following sentence with the correct form of the verb in brackets.

Mark, you can turn off the television. I ____________________ (*not/to watch*) it anymore!

C8. Complete the following sentences, by deleting the wrong option appropriately.

a) Sometimes we *are going/go* away for the weekend.
b) '*Are you speaking/Do you speak* Chinese?' 'Yes, a little.'
c) Simona is in her office now. She *is talking/talks* with somebody.

C9. Consider the following sentences:

a) Don't forget to turn off the light when you go out.
b) Enjoy your trip, and don't forget to send me a postcard!
c) I like this room, but I don't like colour of the carpet.

Which of them is/are incorrect?

A. ☐ a, b, c
B. ☐ a, c
C. ☐ b, c
D. ☐ a, b

C10. Complete the space in the following sentence appropriately: 'A lot of people __________ television every day.'

A. ☐ watch
B. ☐ watches
C. ☐ look
D. ☐ looks

Section 1 - Reading Skills	Section 2 - Use of English	Section 3 - Grammar Knowledge
Part 1 score .../5 Part 2 score .../5 Part 3 score .../5 Part 4 score .../10 Part 5 score .../10	Part 1 score .../5 Part 2 score .../10	Score .../10 **Total .../60**
Ho trovato la prova: ☐ Difficile ☐ Più semplice di quanto pensassi ☐ Adeguata alle mie aspettative e capacità ☐ Altro		

Section 1 – READING SKILLS

Part 1 | Questions A1 – A5

Leggi con attenzione i seguenti brevi messaggi. Cosa dicono? Per ciascun quesito, scegli la risposta corretta (**A**, **B** oppure **C**) *in base a ciò che hai letto. Ti viene fornito un esempio* (**0**) *all'inizio.*

Example

0

Passengers:

A. ☐ must remember their own luggage when they leave.

B. ☒ must stay with their own luggage at all times.

C. ☐ cannot let someone else look after their luggage.

A1. The poster says that:

A. ☐ you must pay £8 to see the musical.

B. ☐ the show doesn't start before 8 pm.

C. ☐ you are allowed to record videos of the show.

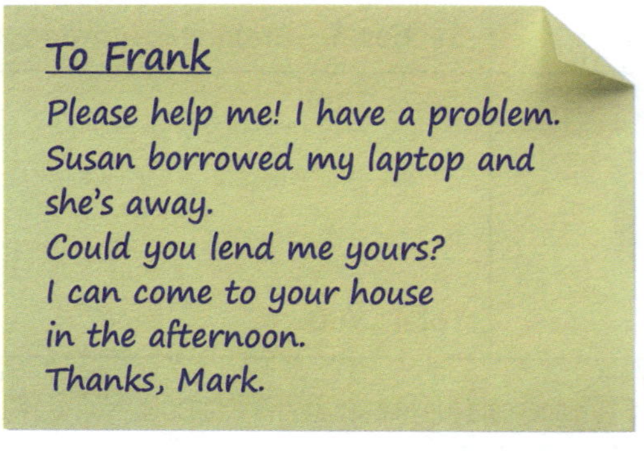

A2. Mark writes a note to Frank because:

A. ☐ he wants to lend him his laptop.

B. ☐ he needs to borrow Frank's laptop.

C. ☐ Susan would like Frank to lend her his laptop.

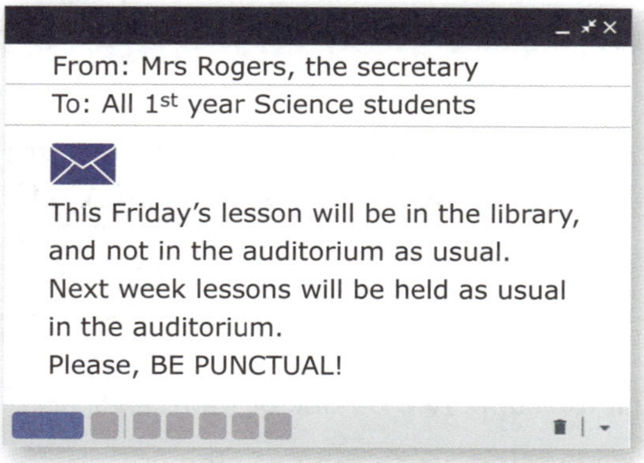
From: Mrs Rogers, the secretary
To: All 1st year Science students

This Friday's lesson will be in the library, and not in the auditorium as usual.
Next week lessons will be held as usual in the auditorium.
Please, BE PUNCTUAL!

A3. Which of the following statements is correct?

A. ☐ Teachers always have their lessons in the library on Friday.

B. ☐ The secretary encourages punctuality.

C. ☐ The auditorium is only used by 1st year Science students.

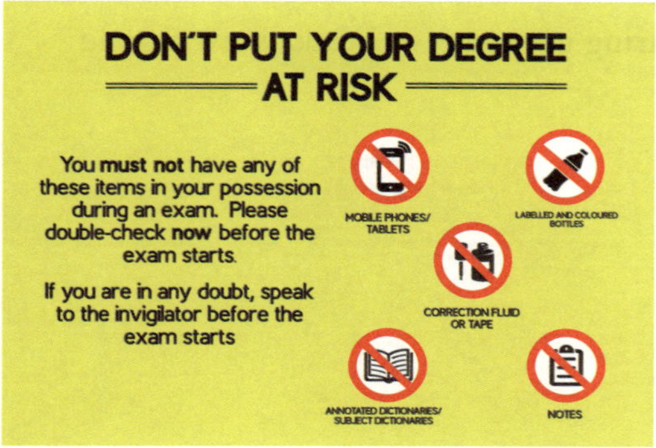

A4. The notice:

A. ☐ reminds examinees what they are not allowed to do during written exams.

B. ☐ tells the candidates to buy bottles of sparkling water.

C. ☐ states that you mustn't talk to any invigilator before the exam starts.

A5. What does this notice state?

A. ☐ If you lose something, you can ask for a refund.

B. ☐ Parking motor vehicles is not allowed.

C. ☐ The management does not take responsibility for loss or damage of your car.

Part 2 | Questions A6 – A10

Leggi con attenzione le seguenti definizioni di alcuni termini. Qual è il termine corrispondente a ciascuna definizione? Associa le definizioni **A6 – A10** *con i termini* **A – G**. *Ci sono due termini extra, che non avrai bisogno di utilizzare.*

A6. ☐ It's an article of furniture consisting of a flat top supported on one or more legs.

A7. ☐ A person whose occupation is the making, mending, or altering of clothes.

A8. ☐ It's a container for water or other cleaning liquid.

A9. ☐ It's a musical instrument with black and white keys.

A10. ☐ It's a piece of jewellery consisting of a string of stones or beads worn around the neck.

A. Star.

B. Piano.

C. Tailor.

D. Bathtub.

E. Television.

F. Table.

G. Necklace.

Part 3 | Questions A11 – A15

Leggi con attenzione le seguenti cinque brevi conversazioni. Per ciascuna di esse, scegli poi il completamento corretto (**A**, **B** *oppure* **C**) *in base a ciò che hai letto. Ti viene fornito un esempio* (**0**) *all'inizio.*

Example

0

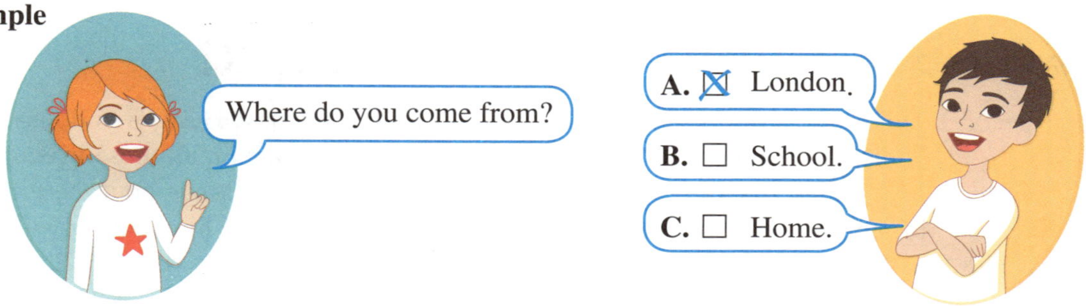

A11. Would you prefer lemonade or orange juice?

A. ☐ Have you got anything else?
B. ☐ Are you sure?
C. ☐ If you like it.

A12. Are you sure they've gone?

A. ☐ They left hours ago.
B. ☐ Never mind.
C. ☐ Yes, I agree with you.

A13. What time will you get to the station?

A. ☐ It's five o'clock!
B. ☐ Twenty minutes ago.
C. ☐ In half an hour!

A14. What is your bedroom like?

A. ☐ She would like some soap.
B. ☐ They sometimes sleep there.
C. ☐ Quite big.

A15. How long have you studied French?

A. ☐ I have lots of French homework.
B. ☐ Since I was ten.
C. ☐ It's on Mondays and Fridays.

Part 4 | Questions A16 – A25

*Leggi con attenzione il brano seguente e le relative domande. Per ciascun quesito, scegli poi la risposta corretta (**A**, **B**, **C** oppure **D**) in base a ciò che hai letto.*

Love is blind

This is the story of Deshi and a beautiful girl. One day, Deshi was doing his English homework but he was finding it difficult to concentrate on all those irregular verbs he had to learn for the next day. He just couldn't stop thinking about the girl who lived in the building opposite and her beautiful eyes. He put his book down, opened his bedroom window and looked across the street. Her window was open too and he could hear her playing some classical music on the piano. It sounded sad. 'She's really good,' thought Deshi, 'but she probably hates it when I play rock music on my guitar!'

The next morning, Deshi woke up late and **ran out** of the house just as the bus was leaving. He was going to be late again and his teacher would certainly not be happy. Then suddenly he saw her… the girl from the opposite building. She was sitting in her dad's car with the window open. He **dropped** his schoolbag and waved at her, but she just looked at him with her green eyes. He'd never seen anyone so beautiful before. But she had just stared at him as if he didn't exist and Deshi couldn't understand why. Angry and embarrassed, he picked up his bag and ran home. As he was crossing the park near his street, he started thinking about his dad who had died three years earlier, and about how he missed his old school back in Shanghai and all his friends. Suddenly he saw her again sitting on a bench with her dog. He thought she had seen him and he didn't know what to do, so he smiled and waved at her but she just ignored him again. 'What an idiot I am!' he thought to himself.

That evening while he was doing his homework again, his mum came into the room holding a letter. 'This letter arrived this morning' she said 'but it's for the building opposite. Can you **take it across** while I'm making dinner?' 'OK, mum!' he said. So Deshi left the house and headed to the building opposite. He wasn't feeling very happy. Life had been difficult since his dad had died. Mum was always working, school was really difficult and he had no friends in Boston.

As he arrived at the building, the door suddenly opened and there she was coming down the steps. At that moment, she dropped something and it bounced down the steps, stopping at Deshi's feet. As he bent down and **picked it up**, she said a frightened 'Hello? Who's there?' Deshi didn't understand but managed to stutter, 'Er, I live across the street. Are you OK?' 'Oh hi, I'm Lucy. Are you the boy who plays the guitar?' she asked 'I really like your music.' Deshi couldn't believe what she was saying and when he looked more closely he saw that she was holding a white stick. She was blind.

GLOSSARY

to run out (v) affrettarsi
to drop (v) lasciar cadere
to take [it] across (v) portare
to pick [it] up (v) raccogliere (da terra)

A16. Deshi:

A. ☐ is a teenage boy from Singapore.
B. ☐ is 15 years old.
C. ☐ is an orphan.
D. ☐ plays the guitar.

A17. One day, Deshi could not stop thinking about the girl in the building opposite and her beautiful:

....

A18. Are the following statements **true** or **false**? Tick as appropriate.

		True	False
a	Lucy likes dogs.		
b	Lucy plays classical music.		
c	Deshi is usually late for school.		

A19. One morning:

A. ☐ Deshi got up really early.
B. ☐ Deshi was sitting in his dad's car.
C. ☐ Deshi missed the bus.
D. ☐ Deshi couldn't sleep well.

A20. The term 'waved' (line 11) means:

A. ☐ persist.
B. ☐ gesticulate.
C. ☐ untwist.
D. ☐ straighten.

A21. While he was going back home, Deshi:

A. ☐ started to think about his dad.
B. ☐ felt his face turning red.
C. ☐ couldn't move.
D. ☐ smiled at Lucy.

A22. While going down to the street, Deshi:

A. ☐ missed his father.
B. ☐ wasn't very happy.
C. ☐ felt happy about his new life there.
D. ☐ thought about his new friends.

A23. The word 'it' (line 27) refers to:

A. ☐ the letter.
B. ☐ something dropped by Lucy.
C. ☐ Deshi's foot.
D. ☐ Deshi's guitar.

A24. Are the following statements **true** or **false**? Tick as appropriate.

		True	**False**
a	Lucy goes to school by bus.		
b	Deshi's dad died three years ago.		
c	Deshi hates rock music.		

A25. The text above is most probably:

A. ☐ a report.
B. ☐ a biography.
C. ☐ an article.
D. ☐ an extract from a novel.

Part 5 | Questions A26 – A35

Leggi con attenzione il brano seguente sull'evoluzione della lingua inglese. Indica poi se le affermazioni **A26** – **A35** *sono vere 'True'* (**A**), *false 'False'* (**B**) *o non menzionate dal testo 'Doesn't say'* (**C**).

LANGUAGE EVOLUTION

Language is constantly changing and evolving, no more so than the English language which is used around the world. English is actually a collection and reinvention of other languages such as Latin and Greek, as well as the romance languages of Europe. However, when people use English slang, for example, the English language is extended and modified with even more new words and phrases.

As generations pass, the words and language used by young people in the UK today is often very different to those used by their parents and grandparents. TV and music also have a big impact on their language, especially as UK singers often sing with American accents without even realising. The English dictionary is also in a constant state of evolution with new words, phrases and expressions being added every year. Young people use a lot of this language, as new words come and go like fashions. Not all slang words or expressions disappear out of the language, however, as sometimes they are so absorbed into the English language that it's no longer pure slang, but a mainstream expression. What about these words? Have you heard of them? Do you know what they mean?

British slang dictionary	
Cheers	It can be used as a toast or as a way of saying thank you, or as the signature to emails.
Ace	Excellent or wonderful.
Knackered	Exhausted, tired, also something old or broken.
Scrummy	Something that is delicious.

Young people often use slang to try to make themselves stand out from younger children or their parents, and also to some extent in an attempt to create a code language that perhaps their teachers won't understand. Words are now also spread by social media, music and TV or video games. Not everybody uses slang and not everybody likes it. A school in Sheffield, in the north of England, for example, recently asked its students to stop using slang words such as *hiya* (hello), *cheers* and *ta* (both mean thank you). It can also be difficult for non-native speakers to understand. However, English language learners perhaps shouldn't worry too much about communicating with native speakers, as research shows that most of the English spoken in the world today is spoken between non-native speakers of the language. But don't give up on slang, as it can be very useful if you watch films or TV in English, read magazines in English, chat online in English or are interested in English song lyrics.

A26. The language young people in the UK use is often very different to that used by adults.
A. ☐ true **B.** ☐ false **C.** ☐ doesn't say

A27. Sometimes British singers don't notice that they sound like Americans.
A. ☐ true **B.** ☐ false **C.** ☐ doesn't say

A28. Teachers have completed a list of modern British slang, which they update every month.
A. ☐ true **B.** ☐ false **C.** ☐ doesn't say

A29. The English dictionary always stays the same.
A. ☐ true **B.** ☐ false **C.** ☐ doesn't say

A30. A head teacher in the north of England thinks using slang can prevent pupils achieving their goals.
A. ☐ true **B.** ☐ false **C.** ☐ doesn't say

A31. Today, most people in the world mainly speak English with people whose mother tongue is English.
A. ☐ true **B.** ☐ false **C.** ☐ doesn't say

A32. The expression *Cheers* can be used as a toast or as a thank you.
A. ☐ true **B.** ☐ false **C.** ☐ doesn't say

A33. You could have some problems understanding films, TV programmes or songs in English if you don't understand British slang.
A. ☐ true **B.** ☐ false **C.** ☐ doesn't say

A34. A lot of English words derive from Latin.
A. ☐ true **B.** ☐ false **C.** ☐ doesn't say

A35. You must study as many slang expressions as possible to speak English fluently.
A. ☐ true **B.** ☐ false **C.** ☐ doesn't say

Section 2 – USE OF ENGLISH

Part 1 | Questions B1 – B5

*Leggi con attenzione il brano seguente sui giochi olimpici. Per ciascuno spazio, scegli poi il giusto completamento (**A**, **B** oppure **C**) in base a ciò che hai letto. Ti viene fornito un esempio (**0**) all'inizio del testo.*

Example

0 **A.** ☒ biggest **B.** ☐ highest **C.** ☐ deepest

THE OLYMPIC GAMES

In Ancient Greece the Olympic Games were the **(0)** .... sporting event. The Olympic Games started about three thousand years ago in Olympia, in south west of Greece. Around 50,000 people came **(B1)** .... across the Mediterranean every four years not only to watch them but also to take part in them. The ancient games were also a religious festival, held in honour of Zeus, the king of the gods.

The **(B2)** .... didn't receive gold, silver or bronze medals as they did not compete for money but to honour Zeus. They received a wreath of leaves and a hero's welcome back home. Olympia was a centre of culture, politics and religion, as well **(B3)** .... a centre of sport.

For the athletes this was a time to concentrate and prepare for the **(B4)** .... and many young challengers looked for support from the gods. Local priests acted as judges taking up special positions in a judge's stand.

The athletes knew that they could obtain immortal fame, if they won. Before the games began, messengers were sent out to announce peace.

The main event at the Olympic Games was not a sporting event, but a religious one: the **(B5)** .... of one hundred animals burnt on the Altar of Zeus on the third day of the games.

B1.	**A.** ☐ to	**B.** ☐ from	**C.** ☐ on
B2.	**A.** ☐ winners	**B.** ☐ losers	**C.** ☐ trainers
B3.	**A.** ☐ for	**B.** ☐ as	**C.** ☐ to
B4.	**A.** ☐ competition	**B.** ☐ exhibition	**C.** ☐ domination
B5.	**A.** ☐ race	**B.** ☐ sacrifice	**C.** ☐ fame

Part 2 | Questions B6 – B15

Leggi con attenzione il brano seguente, poi scrivi la parola mancante in ciascuno spazio. Scrivi solo UNA parola per ciascuno spazio. Ti viene fornito un esempio (**0**) *all'inizio del testo.*

A YouTuber's story

In March 2007, a 14-year-old boy named Anthony Robbins was studying (**0**) …for… his end-of-term exams. Since he was bored, he switched on his netbook and started surfing the Internet. While browsing the pages, he found a website called YouTube and watched a video (**B6**) .... another teenager just like him, who was sitting in his bedroom and talking about how bored he was. Anthony was convinced that he could definitely do better than him. So, using his computer and a webcam, (**B7**) .... created his first video blog and posted (**B8**) .... on YouTube under the name AskTony.

When a few days (**B9**) .... Tony posted his first video, he found out that he had 150 followers, so he decided to make more videos to please his audience. He soon became quite popular, and a few months later a famous English TV anchorwoman, showed one of his funniest videos called *The secret of happiness* (**B10**) ....her programme. This made Tony suddenly very famous in the United Kingdom, and it is still in the list of the (**B11**) .... viewed YouTube videos, with nearly 4 million views. Tony also realised he could use his fame for a good cause (**B12**) .... help other people. He organized a mega party for his 18th birthday and he managed to raise £3,000 for charity (**B13**) .... waxing his chest on live TV.

With more (**B14**) .... one and a half million subscribers, Tony is now the most popular video blogger in the UK. The secret of his popularity is in making videos that he himself would want to watch that don't try to sell anything. Tony passed his exams with nine A grades and one B! He says that he wants to go to university (**B15**) .... the future but has decided to try and make a career on YouTube before that.

Section 3 – GRAMMAR KNOWLEDGE

Questions C1 – C10

Leggi con attenzione e rispondi ai seguenti quesiti di riflessione sulla lingua inglese.

C1. Complete the following sentence, by deleting the wrong options appropriately.

'When she *was/has been* thirteen she *had visited/visited* London with her father, and she *was gone/had been* to some other cities with her family on holiday.'

C2. Complete the spaces in the following sentence appropriately: 'The best thing about that city are the ________ streets filled with cafés and ____________ clothes shop.'

A. ☐ narrow; fashionable
B. ☐ fashionable; tasty
C. ☐ local; fashionable
D. ☐ tasty; busy

C3. Complete the space in the following sentence appropriately: 'Mark, ______________ to work in the morning?'

A. ☐ do you walk
B. ☐ are you walk
C. ☐ don't you walking
D. ☐ will you walking

C4. Complete the following sentences, by deleting the wrong option appropriately.

a) The tour guide gave us some *information/informations* about the city.
b) We are going to buy some new *furniture/furnitures*.
c) Paola has got short dark *hair/hairs*.

C5. Complete the space in the following sentence appropriately: 'I am going to make a new table on my own; first of all, I need __________ wood.'

A. ☐ some
B. ☐ a
C. ☐ an
D. ☐ many

C6. Complete the space in the following sentence appropriately: 'A woman stopped me and said _______________, but I didn't understand.'

A. ☐ something
B. ☐ anything
C. ☐ nothing
D. ☐ much things

C7. Consider the following sentences:

a) What's the name of the hotel you stayed in?
b) Your friend stayed in an hotel I know really well!
c) Could you tell me the name of hotel you stayed in?

Which of them is/are correct?

A. ☐ a only
B. ☐ a, b, c
C. ☐ b, c
D. ☐ a, b

C8. Complete the space in the following sentence appropriately: 'We did not speak __________ the meal.'

A. ☐ during
B. ☐ for
C. ☐ while
D. ☐ due to

C9. Complete the space in the following sentence appropriately: 'I am staying __________ home this afternoon. I am not going out.'

A. ☐ at
B. ☐ in
C. ☐ to
D. ☐ on

C10. Complete the space in the following sentence appropriately: '*Hamlet, Othello* and *Macbeth* are plays __________ Sir William Shakespeare.'

A. ☐ by
B. ☐ with
C. ☐ for
D. ☐ at

Section 1 - Reading Skills	Section 2 - Use of English	Section 3 - Grammar Knowledge
Part 1 score .../5 Part 2 score .../5 Part 3 score .../5 Part 4 score .../10 Part 5 score .../10	Part 1 score .../5 Part 2 score .../10	Score .../10 **Total .../60**

Ho trovato la prova: ☐ Difficile ☐ Più semplice di quanto pensassi ☐ Adeguata alle mie aspettative e capacità ☐ Altro

Section 1 – READING SKILLS

Part 1 | Questions A1 – A5

Leggi con attenzione i seguenti brevi messaggi. Cosa dicono? Per ciascun quesito, scegli la risposta corretta (**A**, **B** oppure **C**) *in base a ciò che hai letto. Ti viene fornito un esempio* (**0**) *all'inizio.*

Example

0

Passengers:

A. ☐ must remember their own luggage when they leave.

B. ☒ must stay with their own luggage at all times.

C. ☐ cannot let someone else look after their luggage.

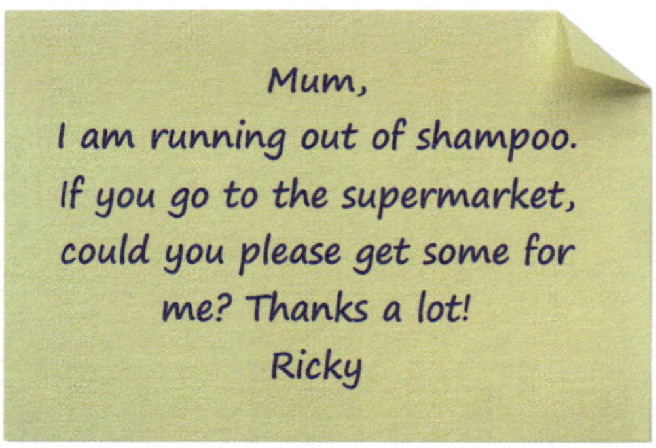

A1. The poster says that Ricky:

A. ☐ needs to go to the supermarket to buy some shampoo.

B. ☐ will need another bottle of shampoo soon and hopes his mother will buy some.

C. ☐ and his mother went to the supermarket yesterday to buy some shampoo.

A2. The memo says that:

A. ☐ you can't do more than five things in a day.

B. ☐ you have to **go on an errand**.

C. ☐ you didn't pay the laundry.

GLOSSARY

to go on an errand (v) sbrigare delle commissioni

A3. What does this notice mean?

A. ☐ The airport is not responsible for any lost objects.

B. ☐ You can have a free visit of the airport.

C. ☐ You may find something that you lost at the airport.

A4. The guest notice states that:

A. ☐ towels are not washed every day.

B. ☐ if you want to have the towels changed, you must put them in the bath.

C. ☐ towels at the hotel are biodegradable.

A5. Which of the following statements is correct?

A. ☐ You mustn't throw litter in the bins.

B. ☐ You are not allowed to carry knives.

C. ☐ You must help the zookeepers to keep the zoo clean.

Part 2 | Questions A6 – A10

Leggi con attenzione le seguenti definizioni di alcuni termini. Qual è il termine corrispondente a ciascuna definizione? Associa le definizioni **A6 – A10** *con i termini* **A – G***. Ci sono due termini extra, che non avrai bisogno di utilizzare.*

A6. ☐ People who like watching football often go to this place.

A7. ☐ It's a portable electronic device used for reading books and other materials in digital form.

A8. ☐ It's the abrupt, harsh, explosive cry of a dog.

A9. ☐ It's a one-piece garment for the lower part of the body and the legs.

A10. ☐ A person who is the commander of a merchant vessel.

A. Click.

B. Carpenter.

C. E-reader.

D. Tights.

E. Captain.

F. Bark.

G. Stadium.

Part 3 | Questions A11 – A15

*Leggi con attenzione le seguenti cinque brevi conversazioni. Per ciascuna di esse, scegli poi il completamento corretto (***A***,* **B** *oppure* **C***) in base a ciò che hai letto. Ti viene fornito un esempio (***0***) all'inizio.*

Example

0

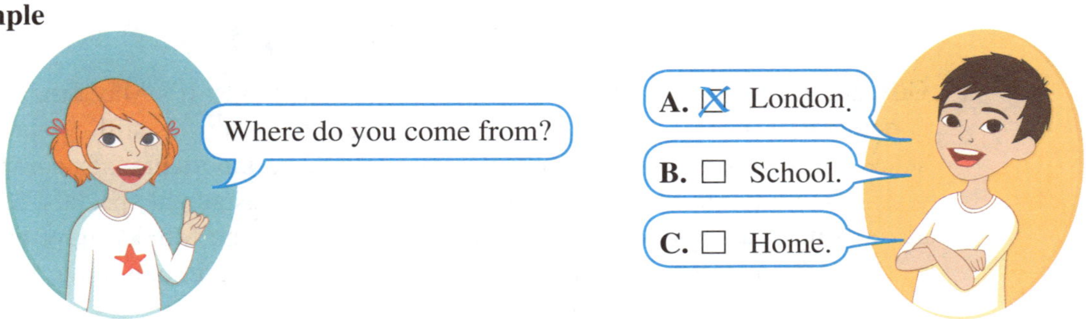

A11. When are you meeting your friends?

A. ☐ I love the cinema.
B. ☐ It was yesterday.
C. ☐ In the afternoon.

A12. How did the woman travel to Scotland?

A. ☐ By bus.
B. ☐ She travelled with her son.
C. ☐ It rained all day.

A13. What was in the stolen handbag?

A. ☐ She prefers rucksacks.
B. ☐ I didn't steal anything!
C. ☐ My credit card.

A14. What will Mark take to the club with him?

A. ☐ He doesn't play soccer.
B. ☐ Some drinks.
C. ☐ He is a champion.

A15. What will David take to the club with him?

A. ☐ Sorry, I forgot to ask.
B. ☐ It's Anne speaking.
C. ☐ I don't know your name.

Part 4 | Questions A16 – A25

*Leggi con attenzione il brano seguente e le relative domande. Per ciascun quesito, scegli poi la risposta corretta (**A**, **B**, **C** oppure **D**) in base a ciò che hai letto.*

Cinco de Mayo

Guacamole and fajitas. Mexican flags and mariachi bands. It's May 5th, and America is celebrating *Cinco de Mayo* – but why? This special day is still celebrated in two states of Mexico, but the local **tributes** appear to be unimportant when compared to the giant celebration in the United States, complete with restaurant specials, high-volume advertising and endless promotion. The United States and Mexico have had complex relations for a long time, but the two countries are united in one thing, and that's the celebration called *Cinco de Mayo*.

Cinco de Mayo is Spanish for 'fifth of May.' It **commemorates** the victory of the Mexicans over the French at the Battle of Puebla on May 5th, 1862. The battle was part of the French-Mexican war of 1861 to 1867. The Mexicans won the battle, but lost the war. However, because the French had 2,000 more troops than the Mexicans at Puebla, it was a **source** of enormous pride for them – and still is today! Four days after the battle, on May 9th, 1862, the President of Mexico, Benito Juárez, declared the anniversary of the battle a national holiday.

Today, *Cinco de Mayo* is a holiday in the states of Puebla and Veracruz in Mexico. And since the 1950s, it has been celebrated in many US cities, where it became really popular in the 1980s.

In Mexico, *Cinco de Mayo* continues to be a celebration of the anniversary of the Battle of Puebla. But in the United States, it has evolved into a celebration of Mexican culture and **heritage**. There are hundreds of events around the country. Many of them have traditional Mexican music, dancing and food. And many schools have special events to educate students about the day's historical significance. People sometimes confuse *Cinco de Mayo* with Mexican Independence Day. But that's another celebration, on September 16th.

Felices fiestas!

GLOSSARY

tributes (n) celebrazioni
to commemorate (v) commemorare
source (n) fonte, motivo
heritage (n) patrimonio

A16. On May 5th in Mexico:

A. ☐ you can eat guacamole and fajitas.
B. ☐ it's celebrated a religious festival.
C. ☐ you usually go to the restaurant.
D. ☐ you stay at home.

A17. Even if the United States and Mexico have had complex relations for a long time, the two countries are united by a:

....

A18. Cinco de Mayo:

A. ☐ is a date.
B. ☐ is a summer celebration.
C. ☐ was established in 1863.
D. ☐ commemorates the victory of the French over the Mexicans.

A19. Are the following statements **true** or **false**? Tick as appropriate.

		True	False
a	The Battle of Puebla took place on May 5th, 1862.		
b	The Battle of Puebla was part of the French-Mexican war from 1861 to 1867.		
c	The Mexicans won the war, but lost the Battle of Puebla.		

A20. The French:

A. ☐ had 2,000 less troops than Mexicans.
B. ☐ were the winners of the Battle of Puebla.
C. ☐ had 2,000 more troops than the Mexicans at Puebla.
D. ☐ declared the anniversary of the Battle of Puebla a national holiday.

A21. The term 'troops' (line 11) means:

A. ☐ soldiers.
B. ☐ multitude.
C. ☐ gang.
D. ☐ company.

A22. According to the text:

A. ☐ today, *Cinco de Mayo* is a holiday in only two of the states in Mexico.
B. ☐ California was Mexican territory until the 1940s.
C. ☐ since the 1950s, *Cinco de Mayo* has been celebrated in few US cities.
D. ☐ Puebla and Veracruz are two cities in Mexico.

A23. Are the following statements **true** or **false**? Tick as appropriate.

		True	False
a	In the United States, *Cinco de Mayo* has evolved into a celebration of Mexican culture and heritage.		
b	On the occasion of *Cinco de Mayo* there are hundreds of events around the country.		
c	Many schools have special events to educate students about *Cinco de Mayo*'s historical significance.		

A24. According to the text, which of the following sentences is correct?

A. ☐ On May 9th, 1862, President Benito Juárez declared the anniversary of the battle a national holiday.
B. ☐ *Cinco de Mayo* is a French festival.
C. ☐ There was a battle in 1876.
D. ☐ *Cinco de Mayo* is not celebrated in the United States.

A25. The text above is most probably:

A. ☐ a report.
B. ☐ a biography.
C. ☐ a review.
D. ☐ an extract from a novel.

Part 5 | Questions A26 – A35

Leggi con attenzione il brano seguente sull'eco-sostenibilità. Indica poi se le affermazioni **A26** – **A35** *sono vere 'True'* (**A**), *false 'False'* (**B**) *o non menzionate dal testo 'Doesn't say'* (**C**).

GO GREEN!

There is rubbish all over the world and just not enough space to dispose of it. Landfills are filling up quickly and there is worldwide discussion about what to do with the huge amount of rubbish that is produced every day.

At the very heart of the 'Go Green' global movement are the 3 R's – that is Reduce, Reuse, Recycle. Whether we are a public organisation, a private enterprise or an individual in our own home, we need to manage our resources in a more sustainable manner. Everyone knows that the earth's resources are not infinite and it is widely recognised that what we do every day contributes greatly to climate change. Leading environmental organisations are warning us that the only way to support future generations is by using our resources more efficiently.

In a bid to save our planet, the so-called three Rs are essential in dealing with the waste we produce. Everyone can contribute. One thing we can all do is start buying things that don't have a lot of packaging or simply borrow things that we don't use very often, instead of buying them. Another thing that many of us are starting to do more often is reading online rather than buying the paper edition of a newspaper, for example. In addition, you should ask yourself whether it is really necessary to print out emails.

We should also think about our use of electricity. The use of electricity can be greatly reduced by, for example, turning off lights when we are not in the room. Whenever possible, use natural lighting instead of electric lighting. Try to use fluorescent bulbs rather than incandescent bulbs, and when you use the washing machine, select cooler temperatures for washing clothes. Another way of contributing is to keep windows and doors closed in heated and air-conditioned areas, and to turn off computers when they are not in use.

Think carefully when you go shopping too. Don't use plastic bags. Take a reusable bag with you instead. Recycling clothes is also a good way of helping the environment. If you have clothes that are still in good condition, you can take them to collection points rather than simply throwing them away. In addition, materials such as paper, aluminium, glass and plastic can also be recycled. Glass is relatively easy to recycle, and so too is aluminium. Paper is a little more difficult to continuously recycle because the small fibres in paper eventually become very weak and some high-quality paper is too expensive to recycle. But think about your paper use and don't forget to use the other side of the paper!

And finally, of course, we should think about the car we drive. Try to buy a fuel efficient car and don't drive it more than you really need to! Many towns and cities have adopted a car-sharing scheme now and it might be a great idea for getting to work in the morning! You should also park your car in the shade because this lowers the temperature in your fuel tank by up to 7 degrees, significantly reducing fuel evaporation. So, as you can see, there are many things we can do in our daily lives to help the environment. Thinking green means being aware of and respecting the world around us, and protecting it for future generations.

A26. People all over the world understand that helping the environment is very important.
A. ☐ true **B.** ☐ false **C.** ☐ doesn't say

A27. According to the author, shoe boxes can be very useful to store things.
A. ☐ true **B.** ☐ false **C.** ☐ doesn't say

A28. Incandescent bulbs are more environmentally friendly than fluorescent bulbs.
A. ☐ true **B.** ☐ false **C.** ☐ doesn't say

A29. It's not possible to recycle aluminum over and over again.
A. ☐ true **B.** ☐ false **C.** ☐ doesn't say

A30. The author suggests borrowing certain items rather than buying them.
A. ☐ true **B.** ☐ false **C.** ☐ doesn't say

A31. It's a waste of paper if you print your emails.
A. ☐ true **B.** ☐ false **C.** ☐ doesn't say

A32. There is a limit to how many times paper can be recycled because it is made of small fibres.
A. ☐ true **B.** ☐ false **C.** ☐ doesn't say

A33. It's a good idea to keep the tap on when you're brushing your teeth.
A. ☐ true **B.** ☐ false **C.** ☐ doesn't say

A34. You can save electricity by switching the lights off when you are not in the room.
A. ☐ true **B.** ☐ false **C.** ☐ doesn't say

A35. Empty plastic bottles are relatively easy to recycle.
A. ☐ true **B.** ☐ false **C.** ☐ doesn't say

Section 2 – USE OF ENGLISH

Part 1 | Questions B1 – B5

Leggi con attenzione il brano seguente sull'andare in bicicletta. Per ciascuno spazio, scegli poi il giusto completamento (**A**, **B**, *oppure* **C**) *in base a ciò che hai letto. Ti viene fornito un esempio* (**0**) *all'inizio del testo.*

Example

0 **A.** ☐ months **B.** ☐ days **C.** ☒ years

BICYCLES

Cycling is a fantastic sport, and bicycles have a long, interesting history. They've been in use for almost two hundred **(0)** .... now, and they have also evolved during that period of time. The first bicycles were completely different from the ones used nowadays, and were not as **(B1)** .... as they are now. Bicycles are always fun and they make it really easy to get from one place to another.

When adults started to drive, after the 1920s, bikes started to be considered as toys and started to be used by those who were too young to drive a car; they provide many different benefits compared with motor vehicles, for example: easier parking, access to roads, bike paths and rural trails. In fact, until the arrival of the car, bicycles were mostly used by adults, as practical and efficient means of transportation. Cycling is also useful to reduce pollution, as it requires a lower consumption of fossil fuels, less air or noise pollution, and significantly reduced traffic queues.

Cycling seems to possess a **(B2)** .... of qualities that give **(B3)** .... in ways that few other sports can do.
It has been demonstrated that aerobic **(B4)** .... is one of the greatest predictors of our physical health and that cycling boosts mental health. In fact, our body simply works better when we are physically fit, and people who are physically fit and healthy are generally happier than their unfit and unhealthy similars. As a consequence, depression, anxiety, and stress are generally lower in physically healthy people.
In conclusion, riding on your own is, on one hand, great, on the other, our best times on the bike often involve group rides with **(B5)** ....

B1.	**A.** ☐ comfortable	**B.** ☐ eatable	**C.** ☐ sociable
B2.	**A.** ☐ good	**B.** ☐ number	**C.** ☐ many
B3.	**A.** ☐ anxiety	**B.** ☐ sadness	**C.** ☐ happiness
B4.	**A.** ☐ exercise	**B.** ☐ gym	**C.** ☐ coach
B5.	**A.** ☐ surfers	**B.** ☐ friends	**C.** ☐ drivers

Part 2 | Questions B6 – B15

Leggi con attenzione il brano seguente, poi scrivi la parola mancante in ciascuno spazio. Scrivi solo UNA parola per ciascuno spazio. Ti viene fornito un esempio (**0**) *all'inizio del testo.*

Guess what?

Today was a really big day **(0)** .....for...... me. The last time I spoke in class was three years ago and it didn't go well. I tried **(B6)** .... say the letter 'W' and made that strange sound. Everyone laughed at me and I haven't spoken in class **(B7)** .... then. But it's been going really well lately. I've got a great speech therapist and I can use my laptop in class **(B8)** .... the time. I've even got an app that turns text into speech! Very cool! And guess what? When I listen to music on my headphones in the background I can speak **(B9)** .... stuttering! That's why I agreed to talk at the science fair today. Our project is about using bacteria to eat plastic. Well, I think it's really interesting.

Luke Williams was waiting **(B10)** .... the entrance when I arrived. He smiled at me. Then Ryan Colby came **(B11)** .... and said, 'Hey, Tom, guess what?' I didn't think. I tried to say, 'What?' and of course got stuck on the 'W' and you can guess what happened then. Ryan Colby and his friends started laughing. So yes, I turned and ran. Very brave! I wasn't going **(B12)** .... take part in the presentation, but then I got a text from Dad saying good luck. And I thought OK, I'm not going to let idiots like Ryan Colby make me feel bad any more. I was so nervous **(B13)** .... I chose the wrong music on my MP3 player. So instead of Mozart I was listening to my dance collection.

The problem is that when I have dance music on the headphones I can't stop myself talking **(B14)** .... the same rhythm as the music. Most people in school have never heard me speak. They weren't expecting a rap about bacteria that eat plastic. When I finished they all stood up and cheered; suddenly everyone in school wanted to be my friend. They didn't know **(B15)** .... my trick with the music, so they just thought I was a brilliant rapper, ha ha!

Section 3 – GRAMMAR KNOWLEDGE

Questions C1 – C10

Leggi con attenzione e rispondi ai seguenti quesiti di riflessione sulla lingua inglese.

C1. Complete the spaces in the following sentence appropriately: 'I don't usually buy __________ in the morning, but I __________ this morning. There was an interesting story in it!'

A. ☐ a paper; did
B. ☐ a paper; have done
C. ☐ some paper; did
D. ☐ paper; did

C2. Complete the space in the following sentence appropriately: 'Jake is really happy: he's got _______________ in a multi-national company. It's such a big change from his old one…'

A. ☐ a new job
B. ☐ new job
C. ☐ a new work
D. ☐ new work

C3. Complete the following sentence, by deleting the wrong options appropriately.

'When Eva White *was/has been* younger she wanted to be *a/an* musician; now many people think she's *a/the* best trumpet player in the world.'

C4. Complete the following sentences, by deleting the wrong option appropriately.

a) I *know/have known* my husband, Samuel, since I was ten years old.
b) Excuse me, where is the *most near/nearest* bookshop?
c) Bangkok is *a/the* capital of Thailand.

C5. Complete the space in the following sentence appropriately: 'This restaurant looks very busy… Is there ________________?'

A. ☐ anywhere to sit
B. ☐ nowhere to sit
C. ☐ anything to sit
D. ☐ something to sit

C6. Complete the space in the following sentence appropriately: 'I saw Tiziana at the airport when I was going to work this morning but she ____________ me.'

A. ☐ don't see
B. ☐ didn't see
C. ☐ hasn't seen
D. ☐ didn't saw

C7. Consider the following sentences:

a) My brother want to be a teacher when he finishes college.
b) We had a dog, but he died last year.
c) Do we have to live know? I'm enjoying myself so much!

Which of them is/are incorrect?

A. ☐ a, c
B. ☐ a, b, c
C. ☐ a only
D. ☐ a, b

C8. Complete the space in the following sentence appropriately: 'What do you hope __________ when you finish studying?'

A. ☐ to do
B. ☐ do
C. ☐ doing
D. ☐ done

C9. Complete the space in the following sentence appropriately: 'You didn't need __________ any more eggs. We had some in the fridge.'

A. ☐ buy
B. ☐ buying
C. ☐ to buy
D. ☐ having bought

C10. Complete the space in the following sentence appropriately: 'Johannes, please don't forget to text me when you __________ home!'

A. ☐ get
B. ☐ are getting
C. ☐ are going to get
D. ☐ will get

Section 1 - Reading Skills	Section 2 - Use of English	Section 3 - Grammar Knowledge
Part 1 score .../5 Part 2 score .../5 Part 3 score .../5 Part 4 score .../10 Part 5 score .../10	Part 1 score .../5 Part 2 score .../10	Score .../10 **Total .../60**
Ho trovato la prova: ☐ Difficile ☐ Più semplice di quanto pensassi ☐ Adeguata alle mie aspettative e capacità ☐ Altro		

Section 1 – READING SKILLS

Part 1 | Questions A1 – A5

Leggi con attenzione i seguenti brevi messaggi. Cosa dicono? Per ciascun quesito, scegli la risposta corretta (**A**, **B** oppure **C**) *in base a ciò che hai letto. Ti viene fornito un esempio* (**0**) *all'inizio.*

Example

0

Passengers:

A. ☐ must remember their own luggage when they leave.

B. ☒ must stay with their own luggage at all times.

C. ☐ cannot let someone else look after their luggage.

A1. The advert says that:

A. ☐ only people working in that place are allowed to enter.

B. ☐ it is not possible to enter the back door.

C. ☐ employers should show a badge before entering.

A2. The message says that:

A. ☐ Benny wants to go shopping with Francesca.

B. ☐ Francesca asks Benny to go to the mall with her in the afternoon.

C. ☐ Francesca needs to buy a window at the mall.

Dear Mrs Davies,

Thank you very much for the dictionary you sent me. It will be very useful for my exams. I will give it back to you as soon as possible.

Yours,

Danielle

A3. Which of the following statements is incorrect?

A. ☐ Danielle would like Mrs Davies to help her with her exams.

B. ☐ Mrs Davies didn't give the dictionary to Danielle personally.

C. ☐ Danielle promises to return the dictionary.

Do not use lifts.
Do not return to the building for any reason until authorised to do so.

A4. The notice:

A. ☐ says to use the stairs instead of the lift in the case of fire.

B. ☐ clearly states that a maximum of two people can enter the lift.

C. ☐ advises people to return to the building if they need to.

Benefits of daily activity

- Improve overall physical and mental health
- Maintain a healthy weight
- Reduce the risk of diabetes and other chronic conditions
- Lower cholesterol levels
- Manage stress and anxiety

A5. What are the benefits of daily activity?

A. ☐ It maintains chronic conditions.

B. ☐ When you engage in physical activity, you burn calories.

C. ☐ It increases your risk of getting diabetes.

Part 2 | Questions A6 – A10

Leggi con attenzione le seguenti definizioni di alcuni termini. Qual è il termine corrispondente a ciascuna definizione? Associa le definizioni **A6 – A10** *con i termini* **A – G**. *Ci sono due termini extra, che non avrai bisogno di utilizzare.*

A6. ☐ A person who cultivates land or crops, or raises animals.

A7. ☐ It's a waxy solid, usually coloured, cosmetic in stick form for the lips.

A8. ☐ It's a tall, continuously habitable building having multiple floors.

A9. ☐ They are knitted or woven coverings for the foot usually worn under shoes.

A10. ☐ It's an Australian marsupial with large hairy ears, grey fur, and feeds on eucalyptus leaves.

A. Socks.

B. Farmer.

C. Kangaroo.

D. Lipstick.

E. Cottage.

F. Skyscraper.

G. Koala.

Part 3 | Questions A11 – A15

*Leggi con attenzione le seguenti cinque brevi conversazioni. Per ciascuna di esse, scegli poi il completamento corretto (**A**, **B** oppure **C**) in base a ciò che hai letto. Ti viene fornito un esempio (**0**) all'inizio.*

Example

0

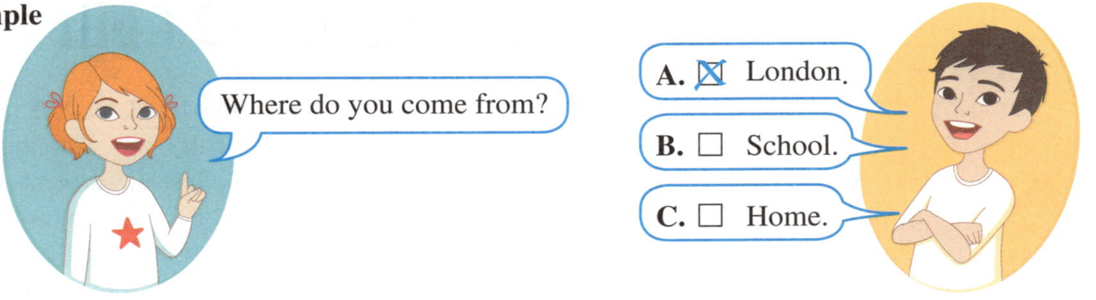

A11. This bag is very heavy!

A. ☐ I'll open it for you.
B. ☐ I'll help you!
C. ☐ This bag is bigger than that one!

A12. What's Jeremy like?

A. ☐ He's got brown hair and blue eyes.
B. ☐ He likes swimming in the sea.
C. ☐ He's very kind and friendly.

A13. What's the programme about?

A. ☐ It's over there, on the table.
B. ☐ It's about vegan recipes.
C. ☐ It costs a lot of money.

A14. I'm really sorry I'm late.

A. ☐ It doesn't matter.
B. ☐ Thanks a lot.
C. ☐ You're welcome.

A15. He couldn't come to the theatre.

A. ☐ I know! He was busy that night.
B. ☐ He will take the tickets tomorrow.
C. ☐ It starts at 8 o'clock.

Part 4 | Questions A16 – A25

*Leggi con attenzione il brano seguente e le relative domande. Per ciascun quesito, scegli poi la risposta corretta (**A**, **B**, **C** oppure **D**) in base a ciò che hai letto.*

The woman on the $20 bill

The American Civil War took place in the United States from 1861 to 1865 and aimed to end slavery throughout the country. Both before and during this war, Abolitionism was a movement to end the Atlantic slave trade and set slaves free. Most slaves were Africans, but there were also thousands of enslaved Native Americans. In the 18th century, as many as six million Africans were transported to the Americas as slaves, at least a third of them on British ships to North America.

One woman made history – the anti-slavery activist Harriet Tubman, and she is about to make history again. Having also fought for women's right to vote, she will be the first woman and the first African American to appear on a major US currency note. The front of the new $20 bill will **feature** Harriet Tubman, as she replaces Andrew Jackson, the seventh US President and a slaveholder. His image, instead, will be on the back of the redesigned $20 note.

Born in 1822, Harriet Tubman escaped slavery and helped to free others. During the announcement of the changes to the $20 bill, Treasury Secretary Jacob J. Lew said that Harriet Tubman was not just a historical figure, but a role model for leadership and participation in democracy. After having escaped from slavery, Tubman often returned to the South to aid in leading other slaves to safety in the Northern free states and to Canada. Along with other activists, she used a special network of safe houses called the Underground Railroad.

Many Americans have been **captivated** by the decision to put a woman on a US bank note. Initially, the idea was to put a woman on the $10 bill, which currently features a portrait of Alexander Hamilton, one of the country's founding fathers who helped create the US banking system. American people gave their views with many saying that Hamilton should stay on the $10 bill. They also suggested removing Jackson from the $20 bill, as not only did Jackson own slaves but he also moved Native Americans from their land.

In the end, Hamilton will stay on the front of the $10 note. On its reverse, the newly redesigned $10 bill will honour another five women - Lucretia Mott, Sojourner Truth, Susan B. Anthony, Elizabeth Cady Stanton and Alice Paul - the leaders of the suffrage movement. On the new $5 bill, however, the reverse will honour events at the Lincoln Memorial that helped shape US history with individuals including Marian Anderson, Eleanor Roosevelt and Martin Luther King while President Abraham Lincoln will remain on the front of the bill.

There is, however, still time for decisions to be made, as the final designs for the new $20, $10 and $5 notes will not be unveiled until 2020 in conjunction with the 100th anniversary of the 19th Amendment, which **granted** women the right to vote.

GLOSSARY

to feature (v) apparire, rappresentare
to captivate (v) entusiasmare
to grant (v) garantire

A16. Which of the following statements is correct?

A. ☐ Harriet Tubman was not a famous woman.
B. ☐ Harriet Tubman is the first woman to appear on a US currency note.
C. ☐ Andrew Jackson was an anti-slavery activist.
D. ☐ Andrew Jackson's image will no longer appear on the $20 bill.

A17. The expression 'anti-slavery activist' (line 7) means:

A. ☐ a person whose ideas are against any form of slavery and submission.
B. ☐ a person who used to be a slave.
C. ☐ a slaveholder.
D. ☐ a person who holds slaves but who fights for their freedom.

A18. Harriet Tubman:

A. ☐ was never a slave in her life.
B. ☐ helped to lead other slaves from Canada to the Northern states.
C. ☐ often returned to the North to help lead other slaves to safety.
D. ☐ also fought for women's right to vote.

A19. Jacob J. Lew:

A. ☐ will appear on the $20 bill.
B. ☐ was Treasury Secretary during the 18th century.
C. ☐ announced the changes to the $10 bill.
D. ☐ acknowledged Harriet Tubman as a role model.

A20. The Treasury Department:

A. ☐ wanted to put a woman on the $10 bill.
B. ☐ suggested removing Jackson from the $10 bill.
C. ☐ suggested putting Hamilton on the $10 bill.
D. ☐ helped to create the UK banking system.

A21. Alexander Hamilton, the first US Treasury Secretary, was integral in establishing the US:

....

....

A22. All of the following sentences regarding Andrew Jackson are true, but one. Which one?

A. ☐ He was the seventh US President.
B. ☐ He was a slaveholder.
C. ☐ He moved Native Americans from their land.
D. ☐ He is as popular as Alexander Hamilton.

A23. Are the following statements **true** or **false**? Tick as appropriate.

		True	False
a	Hamilton will stay on the reverse of the $10 note.		
b	The leaders of the suffrage movement were four women.		
c	The $10 bill has been completely redesigned.		

A24. The new $5 bill:

A. ☐ will include President Abraham Lincoln on its reverse.
B. ☐ will honour events at the Lincoln Memorial.
C. ☐ will honour individuals present at those events at the Lincoln Memorial.
D. ☐ Both options B and C are correct.

A25. The final designs for the new $20, $10 and $5 notes:

A. ☐ have already been unveiled.
B. ☐ celebrate the 100th anniversary of the 19th Amendment.
C. ☐ will be designed in 2020.
D. ☐ are still unknown.

Part 5 | Questions A26 – A35

Leggi con attenzione il brano seguente sulle soap operas. Indica poi se le affermazioni **A26** – **A35** *sono vere 'True'* (**A**), *false 'False'* (**B**) *o non menzionate dal testo 'Doesn't say'* (**C**).

SOAP OPERAS

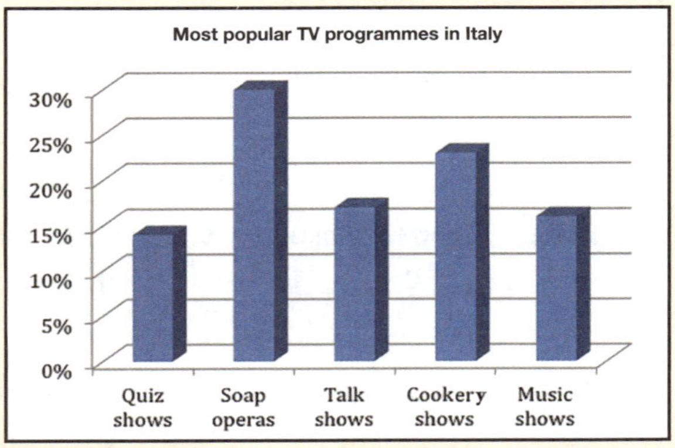

Do you like watching TV? If so, what's your favourite TV programme? Some people love watching game shows, others like talk shows, but the most popular TV programmes in Italy are actually soap operas. In the early days of TV, soap operas were often on during the day and aimed at entertaining housewives, probably doing the washing or ironing. Washing powder companies would advertise their products during the breaks or even sponsor the drama, hence the word 'soap'. The word 'opera' reflected the fact that many of these dramas are often an exaggeration of real life. Although intended to represent ordinary lives, there are always a lot more murders, divorces, affairs, and other dramatic events than would happen in a normal neighbourhood. Several different storylines go on at the same time and continue over several shows, while the same cast members appear in every show, which is usually shown on the same day and at the same time every week.

Soap operas are stories told over an extended period of time, with a storyline affecting several characters and interconnecting with other stories. The most common trait of all soap operas is that each episode ends with a promise for more drama the following day, rather than a neat finish of that episode's story, as you often find with sitcoms or other dramas. All soap fans know the characters well, and often find themselves laughing along with them during happy times, crying with them in their grief, and really caring about what happens to them. Fans tune in daily, almost like the way we check in with our own families. Stories can be stretched out into a few weeks, or characters can just leave home and magically re-appear across town in the next moment. Soap characters can use a private jet to fly between cities, countries, and even continents in what seems to be ten minutes. They can also take the phrase 'they grow up so fast' to another level as they age characters before our eyes to fit into a new storyline.

During the 1980s, soap operas such as Dallas, Knots Landing, Dynasty, and Falcon Crest were shown to adoring fans. Focussing on business conflicts and wealthy families, their sets were as extravagant as the clothes that the actors wore. Soap actors are probably some of the most skilled actors around, as the number of scripts they need to memorize and the hours they spend in front of the camera are relentless. Filming a soap opera requires plenty of improvisation and quick thinking by the actors.

So are you a soap opera fan, or do you hate them as much as many other people do?

A26. People don't like watching TV in Italy.

A. ☐ true **B.** ☐ false **C.** ☐ doesn't say

A27. The word *soap* in soap opera refers to washing powder used by housewives to do the washing.

A. ☐ true **B.** ☐ false **C.** ☐ doesn't say

A28. The word *opera* in soap opera refers to the classical singing you hear in the dramas.

A. ☐ true **B.** ☐ false **C.** ☐ doesn't say

A29. Soap operas have lots of continuing storylines happening over a few shows.

A. ☐ true **B.** ☐ false **C.** ☐ doesn't say

A30. There are usually two or three characters in the storyline.

A. ☐ true **B.** ☐ false **C.** ☐ doesn't say

A31. It takes five months to write two different storylines.

A. ☐ true **B.** ☐ false **C.** ☐ doesn't say

A32. Soap operas are usually more exaggerated than normal life.

A. ☐ true **B.** ☐ false **C.** ☐ doesn't say

A33. During the 1980s primetime serials were mainly shot in the evenings.

A. ☐ true **B.** ☐ false **C.** ☐ doesn't say

A34. Actors with little or no experience play the most important roles.

A. ☐ true **B.** ☐ false **C.** ☐ doesn't say

A35. Soap actors don't spend a lot of time filming the episodes.

A. ☐ true **B.** ☐ false **C.** ☐ doesn't say

Section 2 – USE OF ENGLISH

Part 1 | Questions B1 – B5

*Leggi con attenzione il brano seguente su Amelia Earhart. Per ciascuno spazio, scegli poi il giusto completamento (**A**, **B**, oppure **C**) in base a ciò che hai letto. Ti viene fornito un esempio (**0**) all'inizio del testo.*

Example

0 **A.** ☒ mountains **B.** ☐ streets **C.** ☐ lakes

Amelia Earhart

American aviation pioneer and writer, Amelia Earhart, was born in 1897, in Kansas, USA. Even as a child she didn't behave like the other little girls. She climbed **(0)** ...., yet she wasn't particularly interested in flying. **(B1)** .... she was only 10 years old, she saw her first plane, and wasn't impressed at all. Despite this, when she started to read newspapers, she became increasingly interested in articles and reports about women who succeeded in professions usually attributed to men, such as medicine, engineering, law and management. During the First World War she started to work as a nurse in a military hospital, and some years later she decided to start studying medicine **(B2)** .... university.
One day, in 1920, she went with her father to an aviation fair for the first time: she had a 10-minute flight in a plane, and Amelia's life changed.
Amelia understood that her destiny was to fly as soon as the plane left the ground, so she found herself a female flying teacher and started to learn to fly. She was also forced to take all sort of jobs to pay for the lessons. Then, she decided to buy a second-hand plane, and had to save and borrow **(B3)** .... money to do it. She decided to call it 'Canary', as it was bright yellow. In 1922, Amelia broke the women's altitude record, taking her own 'Canary' up to a height of 14,000 feet.
In 1932, she was the first woman to fly across the Atlantic: nobody, but one person, Charles Lindbergh, had ever done something like that before. One day, **(B4)** .... a storm, she was forced to land somewhere in the middle of a field in Ireland; with this flight, she broke a number of records, becoming the first and only woman who made this crossing twice and alone, and who travelled the longest non-stop distance, with the shortest time for the flight. She also designed a flying suit for women, and went on to design other clothes for women. And that's not all: she also wanted to be the first woman **(B5)** .... fly around the world, so when she was turning 40, Amelia decided that she was ready for this final challenge. Surprisingly, while still flying, the plane, navigator and pilot simply disappeared in the sky due to bad weather. We don't know precisely what happened, but Amelia Earhart is still remembered as a brave pioneer for both aviation and for women.

B1.	**A.** ☐ When	**B.** ☐ As	**C.** ☐ If
B2.	**A.** ☐ by	**B.** ☐ at	**C.** ☐ in
B3.	**A.** ☐ less	**B.** ☐ too	**C.** ☐ enough
B4.	**A.** ☐ due to	**B.** ☐ for	**C.** ☐ since
B5.	**A.** ☐ to	**B.** ☐ that	**C.** ☐ who

Part 2 | Questions B6 – B15

*Leggi con attenzione il brano seguente, poi scrivi la parola mancante in ciascuno spazio. Scrivi solo UNA parola per ciascuno spazio. Ti viene fornito un esempio (**0**) all'inizio del testo.*

SKATEBOARDING

In the 1950s, a new sport started to become more and more popular in California: skateboarding. Even if nobody knows who the first skateboarder was, we know **(0)** ....that.... skateboarding started in a US state. Who were the inventors of this exciting and innovative sport? At that time, in California, when it wasn't windy, there were a great number **(B6)** .... surfers who wanted something to do when the ocean was calm, so they invented the 'land surfing', that is, the skateboard's name **(B7)** .... the beginning. Initially, people made the first skateboards **(B8)** .... home, using pieces of wood with wheels from rollerskates. But after some time, when skateboarding started to become increasingly popular, factories started producing skateboards. There are different types of skateboarding: some skaters like 'freestyle' skateboarding, that is going fast **(B9)** .... pavements or bicycle lanes, while other skaters like jumping on benches, stairs or railings; in fact, people usually go skateboarding in public places like parks, pavements and city squares, and it's always great fun, but they also have to pay attention and to watch **(B10)** .... for pedestrians.

Apart from public places, there are also **(B11)** .... of skate parks in towns and cities: here, you can meet other skaters and you can practise jumps **(B12)** .... disturbing anyone too! When I was fourteen, I decided to try one of my brother's skateboards: I fell several times, **(B13)** .... I loved it straight away and, less than a couple of months later, I got my first skateboard. I have always loved the sense of freedom and speed, so even if I started skateboarding, I haven't stopped rollerskating, and I like both sports now. I also used **(B14)** .... ride my bike a lot, but I don't go on it anymore.

And what about fashion? For me, enjoying the sport is more important than someone's clothes, and fashion doesn't matter, but for many skaters, it does. They usually wear baseball caps and hats, with tight jeans or black trousers and a top, T-shirt or shirt that are popular too. In addition, a lot of them, both boys and girls, have long hair **(B15)** ....

Section 3 – GRAMMAR KNOWLEDGE

Questions C1 – C10

Leggi con attenzione e rispondi ai seguenti quesiti di riflessione sulla lingua inglese.

C1. Complete the space in the following sentence appropriately: 'I have to have this report finished ______________ morning at the latest.'

A. ☐ by Friday
B. ☐ until Friday
C. ☐ Friday
D. ☐ for Friday

C2. Complete the space in the following sentence appropriately: 'We were fortunate enough to visit the Grand Canyon. It has ______________________________.'

A. ☐ many beautiful landscapes
B. ☐ many beautiful sceneries
C. ☐ much beautiful sceneries
D. ☐ much beautiful landscapes

C3. Complete the following sentence, by deleting the wrong option appropriately.

'People complain a lot *about/on* youth and *about/on* young people. I think they have complained *for/since* the past 60 years or *so/by*.'

C4. Complete the following sentences, by deleting the wrong option appropriately.

a) Adriana *had/had had* a difficult childhood, because her father *died/had died* when she was very young.
b) *Although/even* some snakes are dangerous, *most/more* of them are harmless.

C5. Complete the space in the following sentence appropriately: 'Mark's car was parked directly ______________ the restaurant.'

A. ☐ before
B. ☐ ahead of
C. ☐ in front of
D. ☐ preceding

C6. Complete the space in the following sentence appropriately: 'Ski resorts are usually overcrowded: this is because there are many people ______________ skiing.'

A. ☐ whose enjoy
B. ☐ who enjoy
C. ☐ who enjoying
D. ☐ that enjoying

C7. Consider the following sentences:

a) Mary's house is next to the hairdresser's. Do you think you can find it?
b) Do we have enough money to last the week?
c) I am slow to expressing my opinion.

Which of them is/are incorrect?

A. ☐ c only
B. ☐ a, b, c
C. ☐ b only
D. ☐ a, b

C8. Complete the space in the following sentence appropriately: 'You had better ______________ the tourist information office.'

A. ☐ inquire at
B. ☐ inquiring at
C. ☐ inquire to
D. ☐ inquiring at

C9. Complete the space in the following sentence appropriately: 'We saw ___________ wild animals while on vacation.'

A. ☐ quite a few
B. ☐ quite much
C. ☐ quite many
D. ☐ quite some

C10. Complete the space in the following sentence appropriately: 'Joanne and Nadia are late as usual. To be perfectly honest, I don't think we should __________________ them…'

A. ☐ await for
B. ☐ wait for
C. ☐ await of
D. ☐ wait of

Section 1 - Reading Skills	Section 2 - Use of English	Section 3 - Grammar Knowledge
Part 1 score .../5 Part 2 score .../5 Part 3 score .../5 Part 4 score .../10 Part 5 score .../10	Part 1 score .../5 Part 2 score .../10	Score .../10 **Total .../60**

Ho trovato la prova: ☐ Difficile ☐ Più semplice di quanto pensassi ☐ Adeguata alle mie aspettative e capacità ☐ Altro

Section 1 – READING SKILLS

Part 1 | Questions A1 – A5

Leggi con attenzione i seguenti brevi messaggi. Cosa dicono? Per ciascun quesito, scegli la risposta corretta (**A**, **B** oppure **C**) *in base a ciò che hai letto. Ti viene fornito un esempio* (**0**) *all'inizio.*

Example

0

Passengers:

A. ☐ must remember their own luggage when they leave.

B. ☒ must stay with their own luggage at all times.

C. ☐ cannot let someone else look after their luggage.

A1. From this notice you understand that:

A. ☐ only couples have free access to the toilets.

B. ☐ only people buying in that shop may use the toilets.

C. ☐ women and men can use the same toilets.

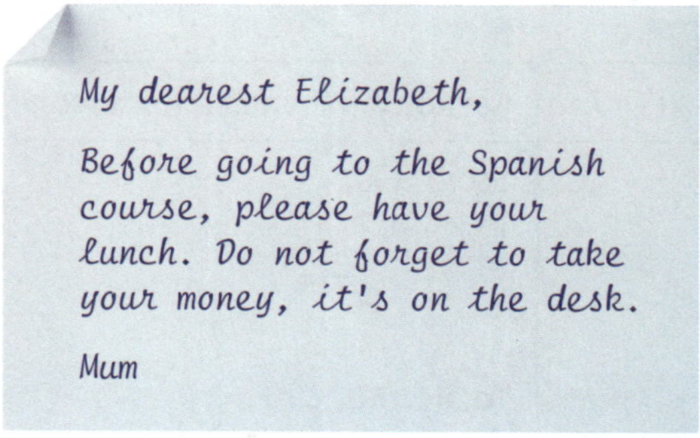

A2. The message says that:

A. ☐ Elizabeth's mum is going to the Spanish course.

B. ☐ Elizabeth is not paying for the course.

C. ☐ Elizabeth's mother wants to be sure her daughter has had her lunch before going to the course.

A3. This sign warns people that:

A. ☐ something has just been painted.

B. ☐ they could slip on a wet floor.

C. ☐ paint is running.

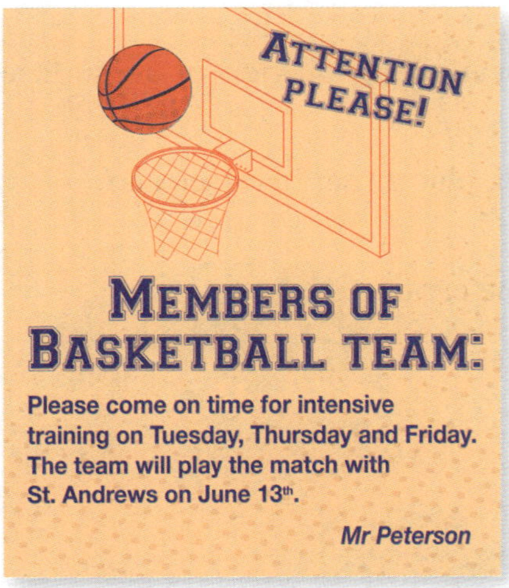

A4. Which of the following statements is correct?

A. ☐ The trainer is asking players to get to the preparation on time.

B. ☐ St. Andrews' players will arrive on Tuesday.

C. ☐ Mr Peterson is the coach of St. Andrews team.

A5. The notice says that:

A. ☐ the lift is broken or does not work.

B. ☐ no more than five people can use the lift.

C. ☐ someone said or did something offensive or unpleasant.

Part 2 | Questions A6 – A10

Leggi con attenzione le seguenti definizioni di alcuni termini. Qual è il termine corrispondente a ciascuna definizione? Associa le definizioni **A6 – A10** *con i termini* **A – G***. Ci sono due termini extra, che non avrai bisogno di utilizzare.*

A6. ☐ It's a large fortified building or set of buildings.

A7. ☐ It's the sixth planet from the Sun and the second-largest in the Solar System, after Jupiter.

A8. ☐ It's the whole body of salt water that covers nearly three quarters of the surface of the earth.

A9. ☐ It's a part of the Internet accessed through a graphical user interface and hyperlinks.

A10. ☐ It's an ornament worn on the ear, especially the earlobe.

A. Earring.

B. Pen.

C. Saturn.

D. Ocean.

E. World Wide Web.

F. Record.

G. Castle.

Part 3 | Questions A11 – A15

*Leggi con attenzione le seguenti cinque brevi conversazioni. Per ciascuna di esse, scegli poi il completamento corretto (***A***,* **B** *oppure* **C***) in base a ciò che hai letto. Ti viene fornito un esempio (***0***) all'inizio.*

Example

0

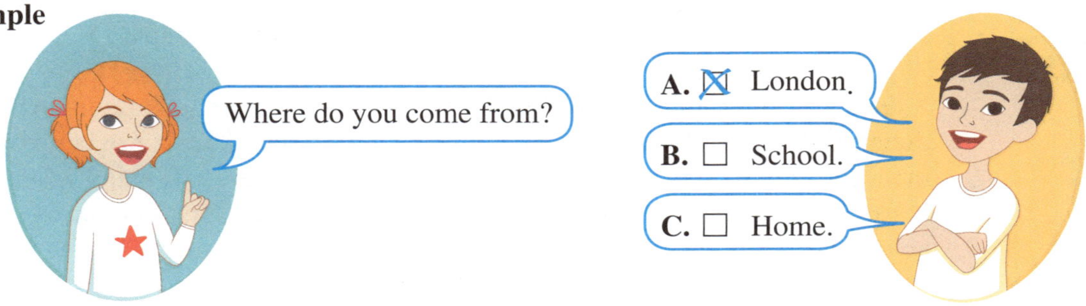

A11. How long have you known your best friend?

A. ☐ Alice is taller than me.
B. ☐ Since we were at school.
C. ☐ She is generous and extroverted.

A12. I forgot to bring some money.

A. ☐ I hope so.
B. ☐ I can lend you some.
C. ☐ Let's go in a little while.

A13. What's on TV?

A. ☐ If you want to!
B. ☐ I don't know.
C. ☐ It might be!

A14. I hate doing the washing-up.

A. ☐ Neither do I.
B. ☐ So do I.
C. ☐ Certainly.

A15. The room will cost £45 per night.

A. ☐ Give me two, please.
B. ☐ That's too much, I think.
C. ☐ Almost five hours.

Part 4 | Questions A16 – A25

*Leggi con attenzione il brano seguente e le relative domande. Per ciascun quesito, scegli poi la risposta corretta (***A***,* **B***,* **C** *oppure* **D***) in base a ciò che hai letto.*

British secondary education

Students from around the world **enroll** at British universities. In an attempt to give their children an even better start in life, many Italian parents are beginning to send their children to secondary school in the UK too. There are many reasons for this, but probably the most prominent is that people have understood that you need to be able to speak English to get anywhere these days.

With British and American universities having such a very good reputation, what then could be better than sending your child to a British school, so when the time comes to **apply** to university your child speaks perfect English and is already well acquainted with the British education system?

There is also a great deal of frustration with the Italian education system. Many parents see their bright and intelligent children **struggling** with huge amounts of homework and constant, humiliating, 'interrogation'-style tests.

The British education system, however, has its negative aspects too, so don't **be deceived**. Fiercely competitive, education in Great Britain is often elitist and discriminatory. Those who can send their children to private school give their children a distinct advantage over other young people, for example.

In 1991, the British government introduced SATs, or Standard Assessment Tests: these are **compulsory** national tests for primary school pupils. At the age of 16, students take their GCSEs (General Certificate of Secondary Education), and at 18 their A-level exams. These exams put a huge amount of pressure on students, especially A-levels, whose results determine whether or not you are accepted into university. In addition, many young people now leave university with around £27,000 of debt. So it's perhaps not surprising that depression in young people, particularly teenagers, is a serious problem in the United Kingdom.

So, before you decide to abandon Italy and its rich history and culture (not to mention the sun!) remember that the grass isn't always greener on the other side of the **fence** – afterall, the British education system can be just as problematic as the Italian system.

GLOSSARY

to enroll (v) iscriversi
to apply (v) fare domanda di ammissione
to struggle (v) combattere
to be deceived (v) essere illusi
compulsory (a) obbligatorio
fence (n) staccionata

A16. Are the following statements **true** or **false**? Tick as appropriate.

		True	False
a	British universities don't attract Italian students.		
b	The author understands why many parents consider the opportunity of sending their children to secondary schools in the UK.		
c	It is not necessary to be able to communicate well in English to get anywhere these days.		

A17. According to the text, many Italian parents think that:

A. ☐ their kids are bright and intelligent, but struggling with mountains of homework.
B. ☐ their kids are not-so-fairly evaluated.
C. ☐ the Italian system works perfectly well.
D. ☐ 'interrogation'-style tests are really useful.

A18. The British education system:

A. ☐ is perfect.
B. ☐ encourages students to study.
C. ☐ is similar to the American education system.
D. ☐ has positive aspects as well as negative ones.

A19. The expression 'well acquainted' (line 8) means:

A. ☐ well informed.
B. ☐ ignorant.
C. ☐ unaware.
D. ☐ unknowledgeable.

A20. In 1991, the British government introduced some national standardized tests (known as SATs) that were aimed at students attending a specific grade of school. Which one?

....

A21. Education in Britain:

A. ☐ does not make any discriminations between young students.
B. ☐ makes use of 'interrogation'-style tests.
C. ☐ makes use of standardized national tests.
D. ☐ Both options B and C are correct.

A22. Which of the following is a synonym of 'elitist' (line 14)?

A. ☐ democratic.
B. ☐ unbiased.
C. ☐ snob.
D. ☐ egalitarian.

A23. GCSEs (General Certificate of Secondary Education) and A-level exams:

A. ☐ are taken when students are aged 16 (the earlier) and 18 (the second).
B. ☐ are both taken when students are aged 16.
C. ☐ are increasingly easier each year.
D. ☐ none of the other answers provided is correct.

A24. Are the following statements **true** or **false**? Tick as appropriate.

		True	False
a	If students decide to attend university in Britain, they will have to pay up to £27,000.		
b	UK state education is less problematic as it is in Italy.		
c	Depression isn't a problem among British teenagers.		

A25. The text above is most probably:

A. ☐ an essay.
B. ☐ a biography.
C. ☐ a divulgative article.
D. ☐ an extract from a novel.

Part 5 | Questions A26 – A35

Leggi con attenzione il brano seguente sui gusti del gelato. Indica poi se le affermazioni **A26** – **A35** *sono vere 'True'* (**A**), *false 'False'* (**B**) *o non menzionate dal testo 'Doesn't say'* (**C**).

What does your favourite ice cream flavour say about you?

We all love ice cream, don't we? It's the perfect treat for any season. You can cool off with a scoop of your favourite ice cream in the summer, and in the winter enjoy a slice of hot pie with ice cream. It's simple to make and serve, making it a regular feature at dinners, parties and other events. When you're sad or just a bit down, a big bowl of ice cream will certainly cheer you up. Ice cream can be served in a cup or in a cone, which means you can take your favourite frozen treat wherever you go.

So you just have one important decision to make. What flavour of ice cream will you choose? You could go for a classic vanilla, or how about something a little more sophisticated, like pistachio? Your favourite ice cream flavour can say a lot about you. Those who like vanilla ice cream usually appreciate good quality and minimalism, for example. It means you aren't an anxious or stressed person and you find peace in everyday things, and enjoy living in the moment.

If caramel ice cream is your favourite, however, you most probably enjoy yoga or meditation, and do a job that challenges you. Caramel ice cream lovers love cats too and their wardrobe probably includes a lot of black things. And finally, we have pistachio lovers who might initially seem reserved, but really have a strong, unique personality who are also creative and complex. Although they might live in a city now, they have always dreamt about moving to the country and starting their own farm.

A26. When it's hot, eating an ice cream is the best way to feel less so.
A. ☐ true **B.** ☐ false **C.** ☐ doesn't say

A27. Ice cream can bring many benefits to our body.
A. ☐ true **B.** ☐ false **C.** ☐ doesn't say

A28. When you have an ice cream, you have to stay seated at a table.
A. ☐ true **B.** ☐ false **C.** ☐ doesn't say

A29. The cost of a cone can be very high if you choose more than three flavours.
A. ☐ true **B.** ☐ false **C.** ☐ doesn't say

A30. Ice cream is only appreciated during parties.
A. ☐ true **B.** ☐ false **C.** ☐ doesn't say

A31. If you like vanilla ice cream, you feel very stressed.
A. ☐ true **B.** ☐ false **C.** ☐ doesn't say

A32. Chocolate ice cream lovers are always open to experience new things.
A. ☐ true **B.** ☐ false **C.** ☐ doesn't say

A33. Coffee ice cream is for those people who like to be on their own, reading a book.
A. ☐ true **B.** ☐ false **C.** ☐ doesn't say

A34. Caramel, strawberry and vanilla are the least favourite ice cream flavours in Japan.
A. ☐ true **B.** ☐ false **C.** ☐ doesn't say

A35. The text says that people who love pistachio ice cream dream of a different life.
A. ☐ true **B.** ☐ false **C.** ☐ doesn't say

Section 2 – USE OF ENGLISH

Part 1 | Questions B1 – B5

*Leggi con attenzione il brano seguente sulla Torre Eiffel. Per ciascuno spazio, scegli poi il giusto completamento (***A***,* **B***, oppure* **C***) in base a ciò che hai letto. Ti viene fornito un esempio (***0***) all'inizio del testo.*

Example

0	**A.** ☐ then	**B.** ☐ there	**C.** ☒ than

The Eiffel Tower

If you go to Paris, it is almost impossible for you not to notice the incredible metallic structure on the *Champ de Mars* in Paris, France. Named after the engineer Gustave Eiffel, the Eiffel Tower, whose base pillars are oriented with the four points of the compass, is the most evocative symbol of France and the industrialization that attracts more visitors **(0)** .... any other pay-for-entrance tourist attraction in the world. In 1889, in Paris, an *Exposition Universelle* (World's Fair) took place, to mark the 100-year anniversary **(B1)** .... the French Revolution. On this occasion, more than 100 artists were asked to submit competing plans for a monument, located in central Paris, to be built and serve as the exposition's entrance. At that time, the well-known bridge builder, architect and metals expert Alexandre-Gustave Eiffel was the owner of a consulting and construction company named **(B2)** .... him *Eiffel et Compagnie*. This firm received the commission but, astonishingly, it was one of Eiffel's employees who thought about and adjusted the design, even if we commonly attribute to Eiffel himself full honour for the monument that carries **(B3)** .... name.
Furthermore, the realization of the tower's final design required more than 18,000 pieces of puddle iron, a type of **wrought iron** used in construction, and 2.5 million **rivets**. Starting from March 1889, at its inauguration, until the completion of New York City's Chrysler Building in 1930, the tower, **(B4)** .... stood nearly 1,000 feet high and that has also inspired more than 30 replicas and similar structures in various cities around the world, was considered to be the tallest structure in the world, thanks to hundreds of workers who spent more than two years assembling the structure of the exemplary tower. From that moment on, the Eiffel Tower has become the location of a number of ceremonies and even scientific experiments over the years, such as the one carried out in 1911 by the German physicist Theodor Wulf, who observed the effects of cosmic rays using an electrometer, to detect higher levels of radiation at the tower's top than at its base. Nowadays, more than 500 employees are responsible for the Eiffel Tower's daily maintenance; they are employed in its cafés and restaurants, they ensure its security, direct the crowds visiting the tower's platforms to enjoy panoramic views of the City of Lights and are also responsible for carrying out a total repainting of one of the most notable structures on the planet **(B5)** .... seven years.

B1.	**A.** ☐ off	**B.** ☐ in	**C.** ☐ of
B2.	**A.** ☐ from	**B.** ☐ after	**C.** ☐ along
B3.	**A.** ☐ his	**B.** ☐ her	**C.** ☐ their
B4.	**A.** ☐ which	**B.** ☐ who	**C.** ☐ what
B5.	**A.** ☐ always	**B.** ☐ each	**C.** ☐ every

GLOSSARY

wrought iron (n) ferro battuto   **rivets** (n) rivetti

Part 2 | Questions B6 – B15

*Leggi con attenzione il brano seguente, poi scrivi la parola mancante in ciascuno spazio. Scrivi solo UNA parola per ciascuno spazio. Ti viene fornito un esempio (**0**) all'inizio del testo.*

An ant's world!

They are small, silent, dark-coloured, and have six legs. They live underground in large groups and, quite often, humans consider them to be annoying; but without these insects, the world would be **(0)** .... chaos. Moreover thousands of species of flowering plants would disappear **(B6)** .... extinction, if any creatures transported their pollen. These silent specimens represent one of the most successful forms of life **(B7)** .... Earth. There are 14,000 species of ants, but there might be thousands of new species yet **(B8)** .... be discovered by biologists. If we consider all these species together, they would weigh more than the world's entire human population. Before humans had even considered walking on two legs, ants had been building their own homes and colonies for millions **(B9)** .... years.

A Japanese researcher who has studied social insects **(B10)** .... more than 40 years, underlines the importance of ants to life on Earth. Ants are very useful insects as they eat small insects and they also remove dead leaves, bugs and small birds, mice and rats from the earth's surface. **(B11)** .... the first ants appeared more than 150 million years ago, insects have established a colony in every continent **(B12)** .... Antarctica. The smallest ants are less than 1 mm long; the biggest can become up to 5 cm, each one having a deadly sting for its victims.

Ant colonies can vary **(B13)** .... a dozen individuals to millions of insects, and in every colony there are ordinary females with specific jobs, such **(B14)** .... workers, soldiers or caretakers. The queens, who will be the mother of all the other ants in that colony, are responsible for the reproduction of the species. Drones, as males are called, are only kept long enough to fertilise the queen's eggs, then driven **(B15)** .... of the nest or killed quickly afterwards. During the evolution, the ants have learned to live and work in harmony. Perhaps men could have a lot to learn from ants.

Section 3 – GRAMMAR KNOWLEDGE

Questions C1 – C10

Leggi con attenzione e rispondi ai seguenti quesiti di riflessione sulla lingua inglese.

C1. Complete the space in the following sentence appropriately: 'Please make sure to water my plants while I am on holiday. If they don't get enough water, they ____________ die.'

A. ☐ must
B. ☐ could
C. ☐ have
D. ☐ did

C2. Complete the spaces in the following sentence appropriately: 'Francesca and Yuri __________ been at the art gallery __________ half an hour.'

A. ☐ have; for
B. ☐ have; since
C. ☐ has; for
D. ☐ has; since

C3. Complete the following sentences, by choosing the correct option appropriately.

a) The teacher told us *to talk/talking/talk* one at a time.
b) I miss *to sleep/sleeping/sleep* in my bed when I am on holiday.

C4. Complete the space in the following sentence appropriately: 'She has been doing the same things for years. Her job must be very __________.'

A. ☐ boring
B. ☐ amusing
C. ☐ exciting
D. ☐ challenging

C5. Complete the following sentences, by deleting the wrong option appropriately.

a) At fast food restaurants, we can buy quite a lot without *to pay/paying* a huge sum.
b) Nowadays children really *eat/to eat* too many chips and burgers.
c) I'm tired of *to watch/watching* TV; let's go out for a walk.
d) I'd like *to go/going* for a walk in the park with Jeremiah now.

C6. Complete the space in the following sentence appropriately: 'Gianna isn't at work this week. She is __________ holiday.'

A. ☐ for
B. ☐ on
C. ☐ at
D. ☐ in

C7. Consider the following sentences:

a) What will you feel if you got the job?
b) If I have a burn, I would put it under cold water.
c) If you saw a wallet on the ground, will you leave it there and walk away?

Which of them is/are incorrect?

A. ☐ a, c
B. ☐ a, b
C. ☐ c only
D. ☐ a, b, c

C8. Complete the space in the following sentence appropriately: 'The burning stick was very hot. He let __________ it just in time.'

A. ☐ alone
B. ☐ go alone
C. ☐ go
D. ☐ gone

C9. Consider the following sentences:

a) As soon as I have time, I'll go out for a walk.
b) If Andrew get up in time the next Sunday, he will go to St Patrick's Cathedral.
c) We are still reading the book that you lent us last week.

Which of them is/are incorrect?

A. ☐ b only
B. ☐ a only
C. ☐ b, c
D. ☐ a, c

C10. Complete the spaces in the following sentence appropriately: 'Pussy cat, pussy cat, where have you ___________? I've been to London ___________ visit the Queen.'

A. ☐ been; to
B. ☐ been; for
C. ☐ gone; to
D. ☐ gone; for

Section 1 - Reading Skills	Section 2 - Use of English	Section 3 - Grammar Knowledge
Part 1 score .../5 Part 2 score .../5 Part 3 score .../5 Part 4 score .../10 Part 5 score .../10	Part 1 score .../5 Part 2 score .../10	Score .../10 **Total .../60**

Ho trovato la prova: ☐ Difficile ☐ Più semplice di quanto pensassi ☐ Adeguata alle mie aspettative e capacità ☐ Altro

Section 1 – READING SKILLS

Part 1 | Questions A1 – A5

Leggi con attenzione i seguenti brevi messaggi. Cosa dicono? Per ciascun quesito, scegli la risposta corretta (**A**, **B** oppure **C**) *in base a ciò che hai letto. Ti viene fornito un esempio* (**0**) *all'inizio.*

Example

0

Passengers:

A. ☐ must remember their own luggage when they leave.

B. ☒ must stay with their own luggage at all times.

C. ☐ cannot let someone else look after their luggage.

A1. The sign says that:

A. ☐ people must stop at the traffic lights.

B. ☐ it is prohibited to pass without stopping.

C. ☐ people can't enter that place.

A2. The advert says that:

A. ☐ you must buy fifty pieces of clothing to get the discount.

B. ☐ you will get a 10% discount if you spend at least £ 50.00.

C. ☐ if you spend £ 50.00, the shopkeeper will give you £ 10.00 change.

Did you see an accident near Bryan Park on Friday November 17th?
We are appealing for witnesses after a Twingo driver left the scene of collision.

New York Police Department

A3. Which of the following statements is correct?

A. ☐ Two policemen have had an accident near Bryan Park.

B. ☐ The Twingo driver left his car near the scene of the collision.

C. ☐ Police are looking for anyone who has seen the accident.

A4. The notice states that:

A. ☐ there are no cafés in the area.

B. ☐ you can't take snacks or soft drinks into that place.

C. ☐ food and drinks are very expensive in the area.

A5. Which of the following statements is correct?

A. ☐ You must protect your feet with special shoes.

B. ☐ Trainers are sold at cheap prices in this shop.

C. ☐ High-heeled shoes are not allowed in this place.

Part 2 | Questions A6 – A10

Leggi con attenzione le seguenti definizioni di alcuni termini. Qual è il termine corrispondente a ciascuna definizione? Associa le definizioni **A6 – A10** *con i termini* **A – G**. *Ci sono due termini extra, che non avrai bisogno di utilizzare.*

A6. ☐ It's a shop that produces and sells bread, cookies, cakes, pastries, and pies.

A7. ☐ The husband of one's mother when distinct from one's natural or legal father.

A8. ☐ If you enjoy camping, you will need to take this with you.

A9. ☐ They are utensils, such as knives, forks, and spoons, used at the table for serving and eating food.

A10. ☐ It's an institution where the sick or injured are given medical or surgical care.

A. Curtain.

B. Hospital.

C. Tent.

D. Keyboard.

E. Cutlery.

F. Bakery.

G. Stepfather.

Part 3 | Questions A11 – A15

*Leggi con attenzione le seguenti cinque brevi conversazioni. Per ciascuna di esse, scegli poi il completamento corretto (***A***,* **B***, oppure* **C***) in base a ciò che hai letto. Ti viene fornito un esempio (***0***) all'inizio.*

Example

0

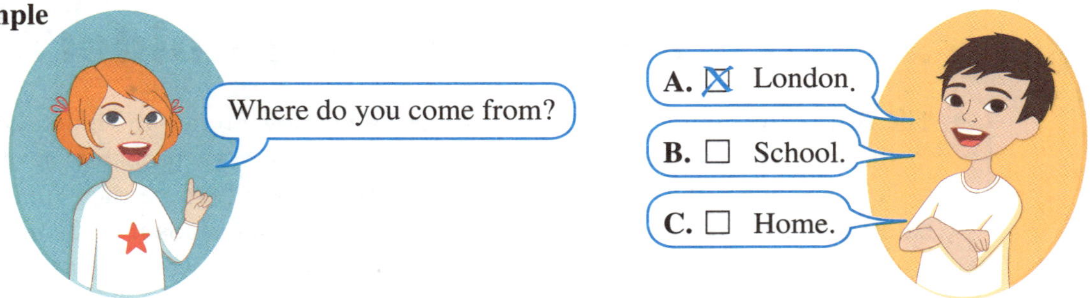

A11. Why don't you buy her a bunch of flowers?

A. ☐ I didn't see them there.
B. ☐ That's a good idea!
C. ☐ It won't last long!

A12. Shall we play tennis this weekend?

A. ☐ He played tennis very well.
B. ☐ Yes, it is.
C. ☐ If you'd like to.

A13. I hope Mason gets well soon.

A. ☐ I think he will be here in half an hour.
B. ☐ Doctors say he is improving.
C. ☐ Mason is very good at skiing.

A14. There aren't any more tickets for the concert left.

A. ☐ It isn't enough.
B. ☐ That's a pity.
C. ☐ It was a great time.

A15. I have to study a lot if I want to pass my exam.

A. ☐ I'm sure you will do great.
B. ☐ Exams start tomorrow afternoon.
C. ☐ Books are cheaper in that bookshop.

Part 4 | Questions A16 – A25

*Leggi con attenzione il brano seguente e le relative domande. Per ciascun quesito, scegli poi la risposta corretta (**A**, **B**, **C** oppure **D**) in base a ciò che hai letto.*

To bidet, or not to bidet?

The British are completely baffled by one French invention – the bidet. Dating back to the late 17th century, most middle-aged Britons have probably never set eyes on a bidet unless they've stayed in an expensive hotel, where they find one in the bathroom. Then of course there's the story of the Italian student studying in the UK, who when asked about anything they didn't like, there is always one aspect of British culture that they have problems with from day one: that is the notable absence of a bidet in the bathroom. Young people staying in host families are particularly afflicted by this problem, as bidets are usually only found in larger, more luxurious homes. For many British people, the bidet is still, strangely, regarded as an upper-class object. Many bidet-lovers hate being somewhere without one. They end up using so much toilet paper it really isn't ecological!

And that takes us to the subject of hygiene. Many would say that Italian households have a higher standard of cleanliness than you would find in the UK. One young British woman with a particularly house-proud mother was made to do the chores when she was young, but even she had to adapt when she first lived in Italy. At her daughter's nursery, all the parents used to meet once a month to give the place a thorough clean. She tells us the story of having to clean a classroom one day. Anxious to make a good impression, she scrubbed every inch of the room. Nearing the end of the morning, an Italian mum looked in and said, 'Oh, Lucy. You've forgotten to do the top of the skirting board.' 'Oh, yes, silly me!' she answered, thinking, 'What? The top of the skirting board? Whoever cleans that?' Italians do apparently!

So, if you know anyone thinking of moving into student accommodation, then warn them. It is almost a mark of honour among many British students that their kitchens should resemble an experiment in bacterial growth! Although things improve when the British students move into their own homes, kitchens in university residences and student flats are likely to be an unpleasant shock for newly arrived Italian students.

So, what advice can be given? As far as the bidet is concerned, parents sending their kids abroad should simply make sure they have a store of wet wipes in their suitcase. In the kitchen, on the other hand, they could try introducing their British friends to some decent pasta cooked in a hygienic environment. It's also a great way to make friends!

A16. Italian students studying in the UK:

A. ☐ complain about the absence of a bidet in the bathroom.
B. ☐ are told by the author to tell them about the aspects they liked most.
C. ☐ have nothing to complain of.
D. ☐ usually visit England for quite a long time.

A17. The term 'upper-class' (line 9) means:

A. ☐ proletarian.
B. ☐ inferior.
C. ☐ noble.
D. ☐ none of the other answers provided is correct.

A18. According to the author, most Italian households, due to the fact that they have a bidet in their houses, have a higher standard of:

....

A19. One British woman:

A. ☐ didn't have to adapt to Italian habits.
B. ☐ had a very house-proud mother.
C. ☐ had a new-born baby boy.
D. ☐ thought that the Germans were the inventors of the bidet.

A20. Which of the following is a synonym of the term 'chores' (line 14)?

A. ☐ Tribulation.
B. ☐ Burden.
C. ☐ Trial.
D. ☐ Housework.

A21. At the British woman's daughter's nursery:

A. ☐ all the parents used to meet ten times a year to give the place a thorough clean.
B. ☐ all the parents used to meet two times a semester to give the place a thorough clean.
C. ☐ all the parents used to meet twelve times a year to give the place a thorough clean.
D. ☐ all the parents used to meet now and then to give the place a thorough clean.

A22. The 'skirting board' (line 20):

A. ☐ is part of a desk.
B. ☐ is part of a chair.
C. ☐ is part of the wall.
D. ☐ is part of the blackboard.

A23. Are the following statements **true** or **false**? Tick as appropriate.

		True	False
a	You won't find many shiny skirting boards in the UK.		
b	Many student kitchens are not very clean.		
c	It's not a good idea to introduce your British friends to some decent pasta cooked in a hygienic environment.		

A24. What does the author say about British university students?

A. ☐ They are similar to Italian students.
B. ☐ They never live in their own homes.
C. ☐ Their kitchen hygiene gets better when they move into their own home.
D. ☐ Their kitchen hygiene stays the same when they move into their own home.

A25. The text above is most probably:

A. ☐ a report.
B. ☐ a biography.
C. ☐ an article.
D. ☐ an extract from a novel.

Part 5 | Questions A26 – A35

Leggi con attenzione il brano seguente sulle razze di cani più popolari. Indica poi se le affermazioni **A26** – **A35** *sono vere 'True'* (**A**), *false 'False'* (**B**) *o non menzionate dal testo 'Doesn't say'* (**C**).

Most popular dog breeds

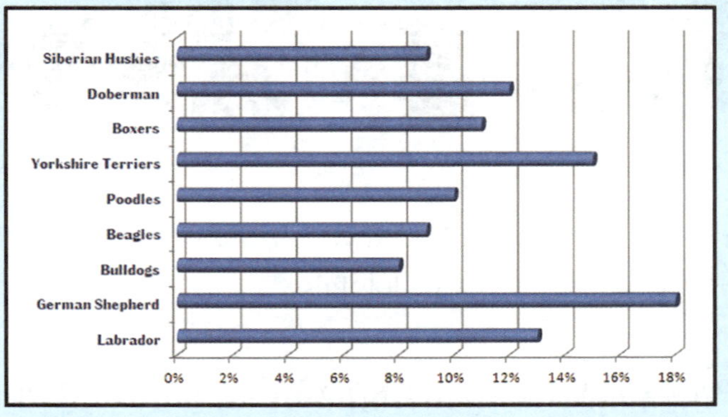

Everyone likes dogs, don't they? But what are the most popular dog breeds? Perhaps it's the Retriever, loyal *Labrador Retriever* which has been the most popular dog breed in the United States for 23 years. These dogs were once used by fishermen to help collect stray fish and pull in nets, and later, they were bred by breeders to help hunters retrieve game. Labradors are gentle and have a people-pleasing personality making them excellent for therapy, search-and-rescue and families. While they continuously seek human companionship and affection, they will also try their very best to please their master. They are of course well known for chewing everything in sight, so puppy-proofing your home is definitely something to be done if you decide to get a *Labrador*.

Then there's the *German Shepherd* which is famous for its use in law enforcement and the military. They are also very loyal family dogs. Or perhaps the most popular breed is the *Golden Retriever*, first bred in Scotland for hunting, and now an excellent pet for families with children. Another possible favourite is the *Beagle hound* which comes in three colour varieties: tricolour, red-and-white and lemon. As long ago as the 1500s, English hunters used packs of beagles to hunt smaller game like foxes and rabbits. Of course, the most famous *Beagle* has to be Snoopy, Charlie Brown's dog in the Peanuts comics.

The *Bulldog*, known for its stocky build and wide, wrinkly face, is one of the most recognizable dog breeds and its name refers to the breed's original use in bull baiting, which was banned in England by 1835. Some families like having a *Bulldog* because of its relaxed temperament and minimal need of grooming and exercise. However, there are those who prefer a smaller dog like the *Yorkshire Terrier*, seen today as a purse dog. Not always the case because in 19th-century England Yorkies had important working-class jobs hunting rats in clothing mills. Only later they became status symbols for English high society. Weighing little more than 7 pounds, they have long, silky blue-and-tan coats.

But maybe you'd prefer to have a *Boxer* dog? Dogs that love to please, in the 19th century, they were used for hunting large game and dog fighting and are now often used as guard dogs. And finally, what about the *Poodle*? Originating in Germany where hunters used the dogs as water retrievers, these dogs come in three sizes and can be a number of different colours. So which breed of dog will you choose to welcome to your home?

A26. *Labradors* are trained as therapy or service dogs because of their loving personality.
A. ☐ true **B.** ☐ false **C.** ☐ doesn't say

A27. More people in New Zealand own *Labrador Retrievers* than any other breed.
A. ☐ true **B.** ☐ false **C.** ☐ doesn't say

A28. Lab puppies love to hold and carry things in their mouths.
A. ☐ true **B.** ☐ false **C.** ☐ doesn't say

A29. *German Shepherds* are often the preferred breed for police and military roles.
A. ☐ true **B.** ☐ false **C.** ☐ doesn't say

A30. It is not possible to find a yellow *Beagle*.
A. ☐ true **B.** ☐ false **C.** ☐ doesn't say

A31. *Beagle* dogs have been used in the most popular comic strips.
A. ☐ true **B.** ☐ false **C.** ☐ doesn't say

A32. *German Shepherds, Yorkshire Terriers* and *Labradors* are the most popular breeds.
A. ☐ true **B.** ☐ false **C.** ☐ doesn't say

A33. The *Bulldog* name has nothing to do with the baiting of bulls.
A. ☐ true **B.** ☐ false **C.** ☐ doesn't say

A34. The *Yorkshire Terrier* is so small that you can carry it in a bag.
A. ☐ true **B.** ☐ false **C.** ☐ doesn't say

A35. During wartime, *Boxers* worked as messengers.
A. ☐ true **B.** ☐ false **C.** ☐ doesn't say

Section 2 – USE OF ENGLISH

Part 1 | Questions B1 – B5

*Leggi con attenzione il brano seguente su un romanzo per ragazzi. Per ciascuno spazio, scegli poi il giusto completamento (***A, B** *oppure* **C***) in base a ciò che hai letto. Ti viene fornito un esempio (***0***) all'inizio del testo.*

Example

0	**A.** ☒ most	**B.** ☐ more	**C.** ☐ than

Little Women

Written by the famous American novelist Louisa May Alcott, *Little Women* is one of the **(0)** .... loved, adorable and appreciated classic novels of American children's fiction. Written just in order to earn some money, the author didn't even imagine how important her novel would have become for American children! *Little Women* is characterized by the familiar and homey feeling of the nineteenth century American home, and also by the extraordinary and historical characters. The story begins **(B1)** .... the terrible and confusing period of the American Civil War, and it highlights life of the four March girls, from their girlhood to their womanhood. The older sister's name is Meg, she is 17, then we meet Jo, who is 15, the penultimate girl is Beth, aged 14 and the little sister's name is Amy, who is 12. **(B2)** .... father is a minister who is involved in the war, and obliged to go and serve the nation, staying far from his house and his family.

For this reason, his daughters and his wife need to work very hard to compensate the beloved man's absence. The story, **(B3)** .... using an omniscient narrator, starts by telling us of common teenage dreams and desires: living in a wonderful castle, surrounded by enormous richness and wealth. In their own minds, the four March sisters have an imaginary castle where they hope, in the future, to live in, but real life is very different from the one they have imagined for themselves. In fact, the older sister Meg, who misses her father's wealth the most, marries Mr Brook, Laurie Laurence's tutor, and lives in a very modest house. Jo, who has a great talent **(B4)** .... writing, writes an innocent novel for a local paper, which receives both positive and negative reviews. It is only when her sister Beth dies that Jo finds the heartfelt sincerity, which was hidden in her soul, that enables her to write a lot of other successful stories. Beth, the third girl, is the only one without ambitions, **(B5)** .... only desire is to practise her music and to have a normal and balanced life, living in a normal house with her parents. Her behaviour, very gentle and altruistic, her capacity not to complain about difficult situations, always having for all of them the right and appropriate words, give her the opportunity to live as modestly as she desires. Sometimes she seems too good to be true! Differently from Beth, their little sister Amy wants to marry someone rich and wealthy, in order to live a life surrounded by diamonds, money, expensive jewels and beautiful clothes. But one day, when she receives the opportunity to realise her dream, she fails. In the end, all March sisters learn that money doesn't buy happiness, and that the real wealth is having a family that loves you unconditionally.

B1.	**A.** ☐ against	**B.** ☐ in	**C.** ☐ behind
B2.	**A.** ☐ My	**B.** ☐ Our	**C.** ☐ Their
B3.	**A.** ☐ written	**B.** ☐ wrote	**C.** ☐ write
B4.	**A.** ☐ for	**B.** ☐ from	**C.** ☐ with
B5.	**A.** ☐ where	**B.** ☐ whose	**C.** ☐ who

Part 2 | Questions B6 – B15

Leggi con attenzione il brano seguente, poi scrivi la parola mancante in ciascuno spazio. Scrivi solo UNA parola per ciascuno spazio. Ti viene fornito un esempio (**0**) *all'inizio del testo.*

The Hunger Games

Nowadays, a **(0)** ....lot....... of young readers love a successful book written in 2008 by the famous American novelist Suzanne Collins: *The Hunger Games*. After being published, it sold really well: in fact, it has sold millions **(B6)** .... copies all around the world! The book narrates a story set in Panem, a city located in North America; the main feature of this book is that its story takes place in the future! In Panem, there is a force that prevails over everything else in the country: it is called the rich Capitol. Twelve districts are dominated **(B7)** .... the unbeatable force of the Capitol. Since the districts depend on the Capitol they have **(B8)** .... produce different things for it. For example, District 12 works to produce all the coal for Panem, and is also the place **(B9)** .... the story of *The Hunger Games* begins.

The Districts, subdued by the Capitol, always rebel against it, and **(B10)** .... stop their rebellion, the Capitol makes, once a year the Hunger Games, as a form of punishment. This annual event forces one boy and one girl, aged 12 to 18, to fight in a battle in **(B11)** .... only one of them can survive. Furthermore, all people living in the country are obliged to watch the fight on television. The heroine of this story is a very responsible girl, Ketniss Everdeen, who looks after her family providing them with food, because her father had died while working in a mine. **(B12)** .... her friend Gale, Ketniss hunts in the woods using instruments such as bows and arrows. When her little sister Prim is chosen as one of the tributes, she bravely decides to voluntarily replace her, behaving as a real hero. The Greek mythology, loved by the story's author Suzanne Collins, represented the right source of inspiration for *The Hunger Games* story.

Suzanne Collins also admits **(B13)** ...., in her opinion, the most memorable story of all Greek mythology is the myth of Theseus and the Minotaur. In this story, Athens is ruled by Crete, but suddenly the Athenians rebel. To stop them, **(B14)** .... a punishment, the king of Crete sends fourteen young Athenians every year to Crete, in order to be eaten by a monster. This happened until one of the youths, named Theseus, fights the monster **(B15)** .... the labyrinth and kills it: in this way, he stops forever the annual series of tragic deaths of his Athenians friends.

Section 3 – GRAMMAR KNOWLEDGE

Questions C1 – C10

Leggi con attenzione e rispondi ai seguenti quesiti di riflessione sulla lingua inglese.

C1. Complete the spaces in the following sentence appropriately: 'If I __________ you, I ______________ to him as soon as possible.'

A. ☐ were; would speak
B. ☐ was; would speak
C. ☐ were; will speak
D. ☐ was; will speak

C2. Complete the following sentence, by deleting the wrong option appropriately.

'I *wouldn't have taken/won't taken* that job if I *knew/had known* about the bad working atmosphere.'

C3. Complete the spaces in the following sentence appropriately: 'When Jacopo __________ to university, he __________ a car.'

A. ☐ goes; will need
B. ☐ will go; needs
C. ☐ would go; needs
D. ☐ goes; will needs

C4. Complete the following sentences, by choosing the right option appropriately.

a) The lights are out. They *couldn't/mustn't/might* have gone to bed.
b) Susan was very upset because you didn't go to her birthday party; you *ought to/mighted/could* have called her.
c) He started his homework an hour ago and has already finished. He *shouldn't/can't/ might not* have done a lot of exercises.
d) Bob hates drawing. He *shouldn't/can't/might not* have painted the picture.

C5. Complete the space in the following sentence appropriately: 'There are four yellow umbrellas here. __________ is yours?'

A. ☐ Who
B. ☐ Whose
C. ☐ Which
D. ☐ What

C6. Complete the space in the following sentence appropriately: 'Hi Logan, did you have a good holiday? ______________________________?'

A. ☐ What was the weather like
B. ☐ Was the weather like
C. ☐ How was the weather like
D. ☐ What the weather was like

C7. Consider the following sentences:

a) Excuse me, Sir, I have to make a few phone calls.
b) There were a few person in the theatre.
c) Your Japanese is very good, Yokimono! You make very few mistakes!

Which of them is/are incorrect?

A. ☐ c only
B. ☐ b, c
C. ☐ b only
D. ☐ a, b, c

C8. Complete the space in the following sentence appropriately: 'Paula went to the supermarket __________ the shopping.'

A. ☐ for doing
B. ☐ to do
C. ☐ do
D. ☐ for do

C9. Complete the space in the following sentence appropriately: 'Beatrice and Simona are very good friends: they know _______________ quite well.'

A. ☐ themselves
B. ☐ theirselves
C. ☐ each other
D. ☐ them

C10. Complete the space in the following sentence appropriately: 'The Rafael Hotel is _______________________ in the city of Nowhere.'

A. ☐ the more expensive hotel
B. ☐ the most expensive hotel
C. ☐ the hotel more expensive
D. ☐ the hotel most expensive

Section 1 - Reading Skills	Section 2 - Use of English	Section 3 - Grammar Knowledge
Part 1 score .../5 Part 2 score .../5 Part 3 score .../5 Part 4 score .../10 Part 5 score .../10	Part 1 score .../5 Part 2 score .../10	Score .../10 **Total .../60**
Ho trovato la prova: ☐ Difficile ☐ Più semplice di quanto pensassi ☐ Adeguata alle mie aspettative e capacità ☐ Altro		

Francesca Basile
Jacopo D'Andria Ursoleo

Sezione LISTENING

› Tracce audio disponibili su ELI LINK

ELI LINK è la semplicissima APP che consente di accedere subito agli audio con lo smartphone o con il tablet.

Collegati al sito www.elilaspigaedizioni.it/elilink e scopri come scaricare la APP

LISTENING TEST 1

Part 1 | Questions 1 – 5

Ascolterai cinque brevi conversazioni, ciascuna delle quali verrà ripetuta due volte. Dopo aver ascoltato attentamente, rispondi al quesito relativo ad ogni conversazione scegliendo la risposta corretta (**A**, **B** *oppure* **C**) *in base a ciò che hai ascoltato. Prima di cominciare, ti viene fornito un esempio* (**0**).

Example

0 What will the speakers buy Jacqueline?

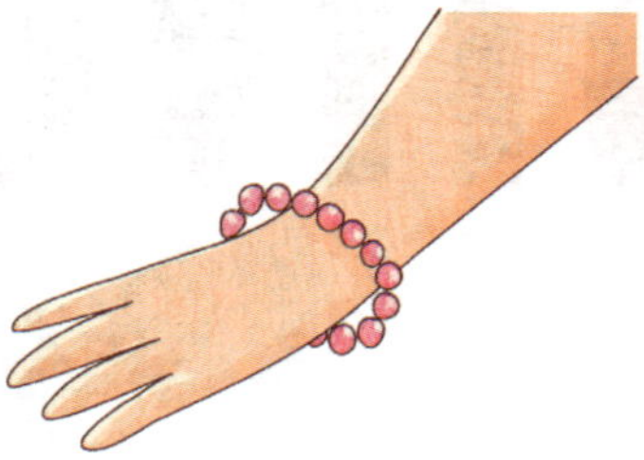

A. ☐ **B.** ☒ **C.** ☐

1. Which is the woman's bicycle?

A. ☐ **B.** ☐ **C.** ☐

2. How many students went on the school trip?

12 10 8

A. ☐ **B.** ☐ **C.** ☐

3. How much is the skirt?

A. ☐

B. ☐

C. ☐

4. What will the girl cook?

A. ☐

B. ☐

C. ☐

5. Where is the woman going to go on holiday this year?

A. ☐

B. ☐

C. ☐

Part 2 | Questions 6 – 10

Ascolterai Lionel parlare con un'amica della sua vacanza. Cosa ha fatto in ciascun giorno della settimana? Dopo aver ascoltato attentamente, scrivi accanto al nome di ciascun giorno (**6 – 10**) *l'attività svolta* (**A – H**). *La conversazione verrà ripetuta due volte. Ti viene fornito un esempio* (**0**) *all'inizio.*

Example

0 ☐ C Monday

Days of the week

6. ☐ Tuesday

7. ☐ Wednesday

8. ☐ Thursday

9. ☐ Friday

10. ☐ Saturday

Activities

A. museums

B. mountains

C. long walk

D. swimming

E. back home

F. shopping

G. canoeing

H. relax

Part 3 | Questions 11 – 15

*Ascolterai Charlie parlare con la sua amica Emma dei suoi piani per il fine settimana. Dopo aver ascoltato attentamente, rispondi a ciascun quesito scegliendo la risposta corretta (***A***,* ***B*** *oppure* ***C****) in base a ciò che hai ascoltato. La conversazione verrà ripetuta due volte. Ti viene fornito un esempio (***0***) all'inizio.*

Example

0

Charlie would like to meet Emma

A. ☒ this weekend.

B. ☐ tomorrow.

C. ☐ on Monday evening.

11. Charlie suggests they

A. ☐ go shopping.
B. ☐ play computer games.
C. ☐ go swimming.

---

12. Emma is going to a concert with

A. ☐ Charlie.
B. ☐ her mother.
C. ☐ her sister.

---

13. Charlie's favourite football team is

A. ☐ Manchester United.
B. ☐ Chelsea.
C. ☐ Liverpool.

---

14. Emma is going to the library

A. ☐ on Saturday afternoon.
B. ☐ on Sunday afternoon.
C. ☐ on Friday morning.

---

15. Emma will bring

A. ☐ some sandwiches.
B. ☐ some cake.
C. ☐ some pizza.

Part 4 | Questions 16 – 20

*Ascolterai una ragazza, Claire, che chiama il suo compagno di classe, Paul, per sapere i compiti. Dopo aver ascoltato attentamente, scrivi la parola mancante in ciascuno spazio. Scrivi solo UNA parola per ciascuno spazio. La conversazione verrà ripetuta due volte. Ti viene fornito un esempio (**0**) all'inizio del testo.*

HOMEWORK!

Subject: (**0**) ....English..........

Name of the teacher: (**16**) ....

Name of book they have to read: *Pride and* (**17**) ....

Chapters they have to read: (**18**) .... and five.

Claire's library card is valid until (**19**) ....

They have to finish the chapters by (**20**) ....

Part 5 | Questions 21 – 25

*Ascolterai una guida turistica dare informazioni su un importante museo. Dopo aver ascoltato attentamente, scrivi la parola o le parole mancanti in ciascuno spazio per completare la scheda. L'annuncio verrà ripetuto due volte. Ti viene fornito un esempio (**0**) all'inizio del testo.*

Heriot Museum

YOU CAN SEE:

Downstairs:

– Entrance hall: (**0**) ....old photos..........

– Red room: Italian paintings of important (**21**) ....

Upstairs:

– Right: there are more than (**22**) .... clocks

– Left: there is a collection of (**23**) ....

Price of guidebook: £ (**24**) ....

Museum closes at (**25**) ....

LISTENING TEST 2

Part 1 | Questions 1 – 5

Ascolterai cinque brevi conversazioni, ciascuna delle quali verrà ripetuta due volte. Dopo aver ascoltato attentamente, rispondi al quesito relativo a ciascuna conversazione scegliendo la risposta corretta (**A**, **B** *oppure* **C**) *in base a ciò che hai ascoltato. Prima di cominciare, ti viene fornito un esempio* (**0**).

Example

0 1. What will the speakers buy Jacqueline?

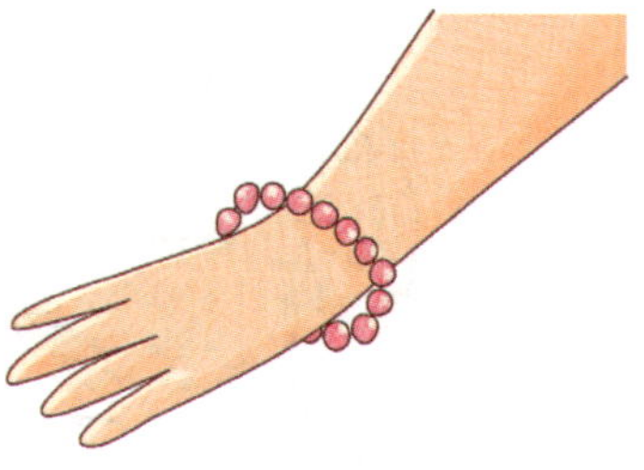

A. ☐

B. ☒

C. ☐

1. What does the teacher ask the students to bring on the school trip?

A. ☐

B. ☐

C. ☐

2. What job does the boy want to do in the future?

A. ☐

B. ☐

C. ☐

3. What kind of film does the boy like the most?

A. ☐

B. ☐

C. ☐

4. What time are the speakers meeting at the park?

A. ☐

B. ☐

C. ☐

5. What is the boy planning to do at the weekend?

A. ☐

B. ☐

C. ☐

Part 2 | Questions 6 – 10

Ascolterai Patrick parlare con sua cugina Bea dei regali che ha ricevuto per Natale. Cosa ha ricevuto da ciascun amico? Dopo aver ascoltato attentamente, scrivi accanto al nome di ciascun amico (**6 – 10**) *il regalo corrispondente* (**A – H**). *La conversazione verrà ripetuta due volte. Ti viene fornito un esempio* (**0**) *all'inizio.*

Example

0 ☐D Bea

Friends

6. ☐ Mark

7. ☐ Ingrid

8. ☐ Isabel

9. ☐ Kate

10. ☐ Richard

Presents

A. bracelet

B. CD

C. sweets

D. book

E. scarf

F. sunglasses

G. chocolate

H. T-shirt

Part 3 | Questions 11 – 15

*Ascolterai una persona parlare con una sua amica di un nuovo cinema. Dopo aver ascoltato attentamente, rispondi a ciascun quesito scegliendo la risposta corretta (***A**, **B** *oppure* **C***) in base a ciò che hai ascoltato. La conversazione verrà ripetuta due volte. Ti viene fornito un esempio (***0***) all'inizio.*

Example

0

The cinema is

A. ☐ behind the hospital.

B. ☒ next to the park.

C. ☐ opposite the school.

11. The cinema was inaugurated

A. ☐ four weeks ago.
B. ☐ three weeks ago.
C. ☐ two weeks ago.

12. The first film the boy saw was

A. ☐ a horror film.
B. ☐ a funny comedy.
C. ☐ a science fiction.

13. Yesterday, the boy paid

A. ☐ £10.50.
B. ☐ £8.
C. ☐ £6.

14. The speakers are going to the cinema together on

A. ☐ Sunday.
B. ☐ Saturday.
C. ☐ Friday.

15. On Saturday and Sunday, the cinema opens at

A. ☐ 7 pm.
B. ☐ 7.30 pm.
C. ☐ 8 pm.

Part 4 | Questions 16 – 20

Ascolterai una persona programmare con un tour operator un viaggio a Londra. Dopo aver ascoltato attentamente, scrivi la parola mancante in ciascuno spazio. Scrivi solo UNA parola per ciascuno spazio. La conversazione verrà ripetuta due volte. Ti viene fornito un esempio (**0**) *all'inizio del testo.*

A trip to London

Full name of the speaker: Steven (**0**) ....McFlurry.......... .

Name of hotel and address: Ritz Hotel, 36 (**16**) .... Road.

Price of a single room per night: £(**17**) ....

Telephone number of hotel: (**18**) ....

The hotel is close to a restaurant that is over (**19**) .... years old!

Restaurant closed on: (**20**) .... and Fridays.

Part 5 | Questions 21 – 25

Ascolterai un annuncio pubblicitario alla radio. Dopo aver ascoltato attentamente, scrivi la parola mancante in ciascuno spazio per completare la scheda. Scrivi solo UNA parola per ciascuno spazio. L'annuncio verrà ripetuto due volte. Ti viene fornito un esempio (**0**) *all'inizio del testo.*

AUTUMN FEST PARTY!

This fest celebrates the end of (**0**) ....summer.......... .

Date: (**21**) .... the 3rd of September.

Time: 10 am - (**22**) .... pm.

Price: £ (**23**) .... per each ticket.

Discounts: free entrance for children under the age of (**24**) .... !

Tickets & Infos: Sunfield Tourist Infopoint, at (**25**) .... Rocky Street.

LISTENING TEST 3

Part 1 | Questions 1 – 5

*Ascolterai cinque brevi conversazioni, ciascuna delle quali verrà ripetuta due volte. Dopo aver ascoltato attentamente, rispondi al quesito relativo a ciascuna conversazione scegliendo la risposta corretta (***A***,* **B** *oppure* **C***) in base a ciò che hai ascoltato. Prima di cominciare, ti viene fornito un esempio (***0***).*

Example

0 What will the speakers buy Jacqueline?

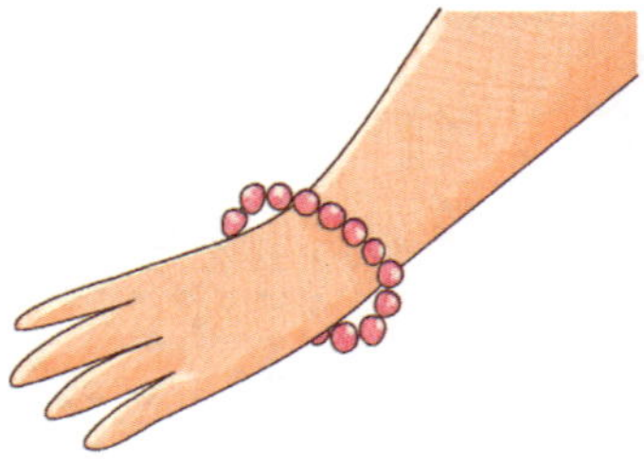

A. ☐ **B.** ☒ **C.** ☐

1. What time was the man's appointment?

A. ☐ **B.** ☐ **C.** ☐

2. What's the weather like in London?

A. ☐ **B.** ☐ **C.** ☐

3. What colour T-shirt does the customer buy?

A. ☐ **B.** ☐ **C.** ☐

4. What do they decide to order?

A. ☐ **B.** ☐ **C.** ☐

5. How far is the nearest supermarket?

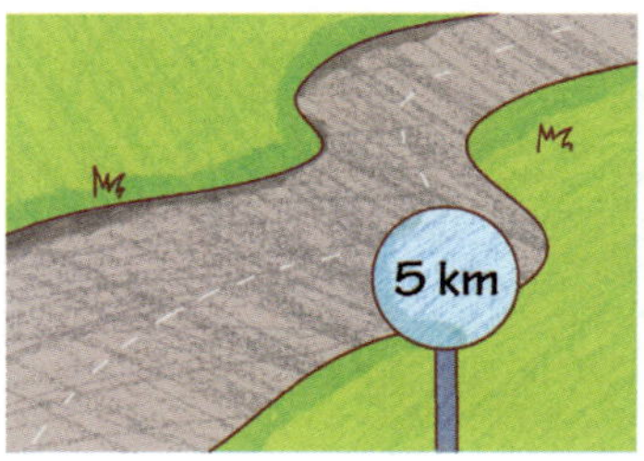

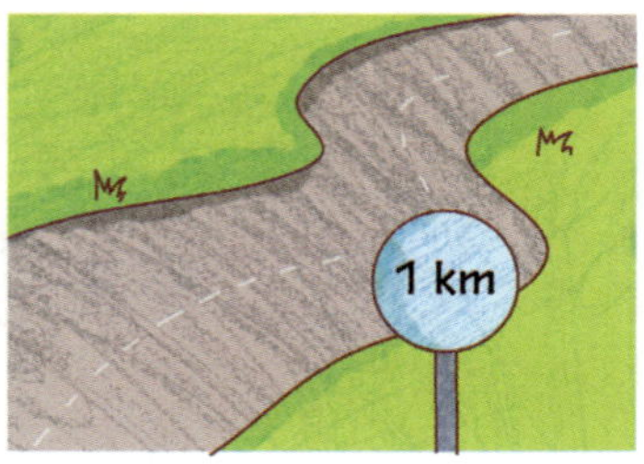

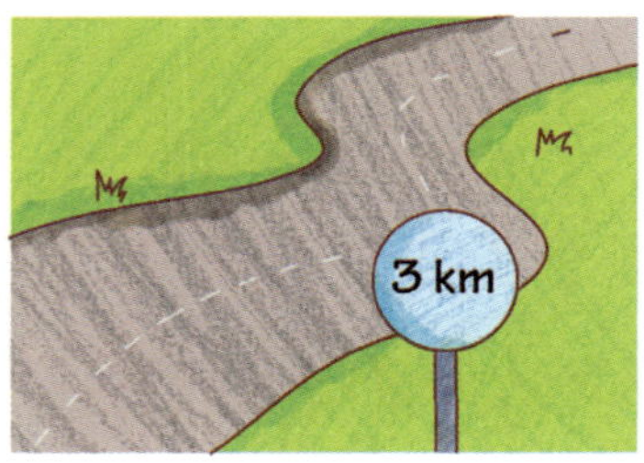

A. ☐ **B.** ☐ **C.** ☐

Part 2 | Questions 6 – 10

Ascolterai un ragazzo e una ragazza parlare dei loro professori e delle materie che insegnano a scuola. Cosa insegnano i professori? Dopo aver ascoltato attentamente, scrivi accanto al nome di ciascun professore (**6** – **10**) *la materia che insegna* (**A** – **H**). *La conversazione verrà ripetuta due volte. Ti viene fornito un esempio* (**0**) *all'inizio.*

Example

0 H Miss Temple

Teachers

6. ☐ Mrs Davies

7. ☐ Mr Simmons

8. ☐ Mr Brites

9. ☐ Miss Collins

10. ☐ Mr Jones

Subjects

A. Geography

B. French

C. English

D. Maths

E. History

F. Physical education

G. Music

H. Art

Part 3 | Questions 11 – 15

*Ascolterai una guida turistica illustrare le maggiori attrazioni della città di Londra. Dopo aver ascoltato attentamente, rispondi a ciascun quesito scegliendo la risposta corretta (***A, B** *oppure* **C***) in base a ciò che hai ascoltato. La conversazione verrà ripetuta due volte. Ti viene fornito un esempio (***0***) all'inizio.*

Example

0

The tour around London will take

A. ☒ three hours.
B. ☐ four hours.
C. ☐ two hours.

11. At Madame Tussauds Museum you can see

A. ☐ old cars.
B. ☐ statues of famous actors.
C. ☐ a lot of shops.

12. Oxford Street is very famous for

A. ☐ tea rooms.
B. ☐ fashion shops.
C. ☐ exotic restaurants.

13. Big Ben is the nickname for

A. ☐ the Houses of Parliament.
B. ☐ the Great Bell.
C. ☐ the Queen's husband.

14. You can enjoy great views of London from

A. ☐ the Big Ben.
B. ☐ St. Paul's Cathedral.
C. ☐ the London Eye.

15. In the summer the Queen goes to

A. ☐ Balmoral Castle.
B. ☐ Buckingham Palace.
C. ☐ the Tower of London.

Part 4 | Questions 16 – 20

14 *Ascolterai una persona prenotare una stanza d'albergo. Dopo aver ascoltato attentamente, scrivi la parola mancante in ciascuno spazio. Scrivi solo UNA parola per ciascuno spazio. La conversazione verrà ripetuta due volte. Ti viene fornito un esempio (**0**) all'inizio del testo.*

Making a reservation

Name of the hotel: Top (**0**) ......Hill...... Hotel.

The lady wants to book a room for (**16**) the .... weekend of December.

She is staying at the hotel for: (**17**) .... nights.

She books a room with a: (**18**) .... bed.

The room has a view of the (**19**) ....

Her phone number is: (**20**) ....

Part 5 | Questions 21 – 25

15 *Ascolterai un discorso di un ragazzo che spiega ai suoi compagni di classe chi è il suo modello di riferimento. Dopo aver ascoltato attentamente, scrivi la parola mancante in ciascuno spazio per completare la scheda. Scrivi solo UNA parola per ciascuno spazio. L'annuncio verrà ripetuto due volte. Ti viene fornito un esempio (**0**) all'inizio del testo.*

My hero!

The student's role model is John (**0**) ......Lennon...... .

He was a member of the band: The (**21**) ....

The singer's most famous song was (**22**) ....

It was written in (**23**) .... and it was about universal (**24**) ....

The artist died when he was only (**25**) ....

LISTENING TEST 4

Part 1 | Questions 1 – 5

*Ascolterai cinque brevi conversazioni, ciascuna delle quali verrà ripetuta due volte. Dopo aver ascoltato attentamente, rispondi al quesito relativo a ciascuna conversazione scegliendo la risposta corretta (***A***,* **B** *oppure* **C***) in base a ciò che hai ascoltato. Prima di cominciare, ti viene fornito un esempio (***0***).*

Example

0 What will the speakers buy Jacqueline?

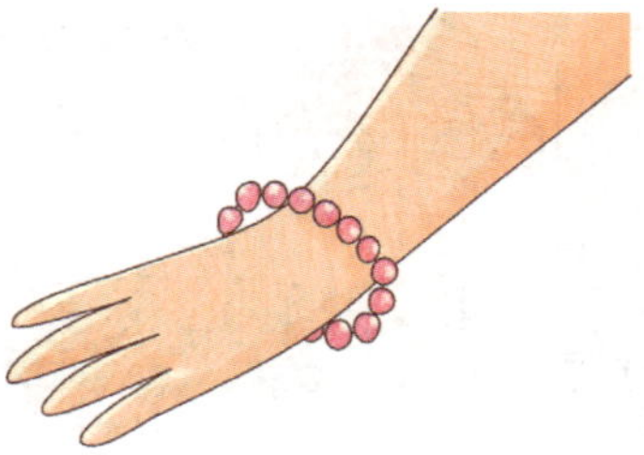

A. ☐ **B.** ☒ **C.** ☐

1. What will Pat do after dinner?

A. ☐ **B.** ☐ **C.** ☐

2. What kind of housework does the boy have to do?

A. ☐ **B.** ☐ **C.** ☐

3. Where are Thomas and Lily at the moment?

A. ☐

B. ☐

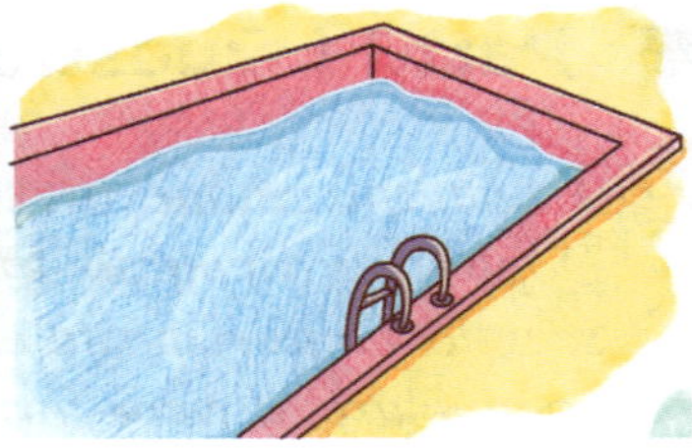

C. ☐

4. Where do the women decide to meet?

A. ☐

B. ☐

C. ☐

5. What did the friends do on holiday?

A. ☐

B. ☐

C. ☐

Part 2 | Questions 6 – 10

17 *Ascolterai un insegnante che chiede ai suoi alunni quali animali domestici possiedono. Quale animale ha ciascun bambino? Dopo aver ascoltato attentamente, scrivi accanto al nome di ciascun bambino* (**6** – **10**) *l'animale domestico corrispondente* (**A** – **H**). *La conversazione verrà ripetuta due volte. Ti viene fornito un esempio* (**0**) *all'inizio.*

Example

0 [F] Teacher

Students

6. ☐ Tom
7. ☐ Marika
8. ☐ Britney
9. ☐ Buddy
10. ☐ Steven

Animals

A. dog
B. hamster
C. rabbit
D. turtle
E. goldfish
F. cat
G. squirrel
H. snake

Part 3 | Questions 11 – 15

*Ascolterai una persona parlare con una sua amica del party che sta organizzando. Dopo aver ascoltato attentamente, rispondi a ciascun quesito scegliendo la risposta corretta (**A**, **B** oppure **C**) in base a ciò che hai ascoltato. La conversazione verrà ripetuta due volte. Ti viene fornito un esempio (**0**) all'inizio.*

Example

0

Danielle organized a party for

A. ☐ twelve people.
B. ☒ twenty people.
C. ☐ two people.

11. She is going to prepare

A. ☐ sandwiches and chocolate cake.
B. ☐ potatoes and cola.
C. ☐ hamburgers.

12. William is going to play

A. ☐ his flute.
B. ☐ Danielle's guitar.
C. ☐ his guitar.

13. Last year her granny made a lovely

A. ☐ scarf.
B. ☐ hat.
C. ☐ sweater.

14. Danielle would like to receive

A. ☐ a CD player.
B. ☐ a hoverboard.
C. ☐ a guitar.

15. Joey will be at Danielle's place at

A. ☐ 15. 7 am.
B. ☐ 6.30 pm.
C. ☐ 5 pm.

Part 4 | Questions 16 – 20

19 *Ascolterai una persona che va dal dottore per problemi di salute. Dopo aver ascoltato attentamente, scrivi la parola mancante in ciascuno spazio. Scrivi solo UNA parola per ciascuno spazio. La conversazione verrà ripetuta due volte. Ti viene fornito un esempio* (**0**) *all'inizio del testo.*

AT THE DOCTOR

Name of the doctor: Doctor (**0**) ....Jenkins..........

The patient has bad (**16**) ....

She hasn't felt well for about a (**17**) ....

She is working long (**18**) ....

The doctor thinks it could be (**19**) .... or tiredness.

The patient has to drink at least (**20**) .... litres of water.

Part 5 | Questions 21 – 25

20 *Ascolterai un presentatore che illustra un video documentario sulle tigri. Dopo aver ascoltato attentamente, scrivi la parola mancante in ciascuno spazio per completare la scheda. Scrivi solo UNA parola per ciascuno spazio. L'annuncio verrà ripetuto due volte. Ti viene fornito un esempio* (**0**) *all'inizio del testo.*

TIGERS!

The tiger is the largest wild (**0**) ....cat.......... in the world.

A full-grown tiger weighs (**21**) .... kilograms.

A tiger's tail can be up to (**22**) .... metre long.

Tigers wait until it is (**23**) .... to hunt.

Unlike other cats, tigers enjoy the water and are good (**24**) ....

You can identify a tiger by its (**25**) ....

LISTENING TEST 5

Part 1 | Questions 1 – 5

*Ascolterai cinque brevi conversazioni, ciascuna delle quali verrà ripetuta due volte. Dopo aver ascoltato attentamente, rispondi al quesito relativo a ciascuna conversazione scegliendo la risposta corretta (**A**, **B** oppure **C**) in base a ciò che hai ascoltato. Prima di cominciare, ti viene fornito un esempio (**0**).*

Example

0 What will the speakers buy Jacqueline?

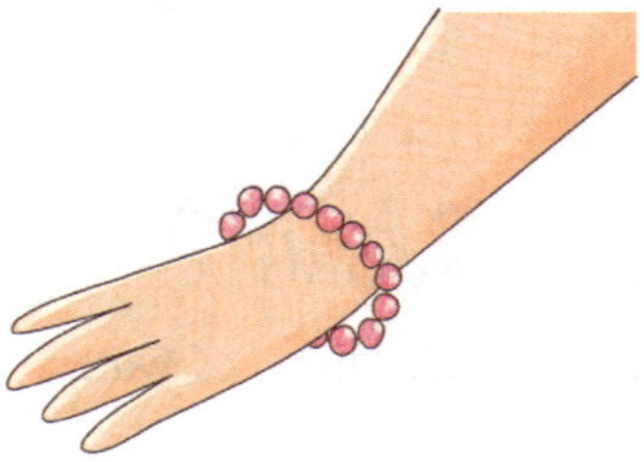

A. ☐ **B.** ☒ **C.** ☐

---

1. Which is Elizabeth?

A. ☐ **B.** ☐ **C.** ☐

2. What does the woman want to buy?

A. ☐ **B.** ☐ **C.** ☐

3. What was the weather like at the lake?

A. ☐ **B.** ☐ **C.** ☐

4. Where do they stop?

A. ☐ **B.** ☐ **C.** ☐

5. How did Ian's family travel to Nice?

A. ☐ **B.** ☐ **C.** ☐

Part 2 | Questions 6 – 10

Ascolterai Mike parlare con la sua amica Ann delle professioni dei suoi familiari. Che lavoro fa ciascun parente? Dopo aver ascoltato attentamente, scrivi accanto a ciascun familiare (**6 – 10**) *la professione corrispondente* (**A – H**). *La conversazione verrà ripetuta due volte. Ti viene fornito un esempio* (**0**) *all'inizio.*

Example

0 [E] Cousin

Parents

6. ☐ mum

7. ☐ dad

8. ☐ sister

9. ☐ aunt

10. ☐ uncle

Professions

A. doctor

B. actress

C. lawyer

D. pilot

E. teacher

F. nurse

G. tennis player

H. singer

Part 3 | Questions 11 – 15

*Ascolterai una ragazza, Rose, parlare con un suo amico dei suoi nuovi compagni di classe. Dopo aver ascoltato attentamente, rispondi a ciascun quesito scegliendo la risposta corretta (**A**, **B** oppure **C**) in base a ciò che hai ascoltato. La conversazione verrà ripetuta due volte. Ti viene fornito un esempio (**0**) all'inizio.*

Example

0

Rose is going to the park

A. ☐ with Jack and Richard.

B. ☐ with Jack only.

C. ☒ with her new classmates.

11. Richard is going to

A. ☐ the shopping mall with Jack.

B. ☐ the shopping mall with Jack and his brother.

C. ☐ the beach with Rachel and Manuel.

---

12. Mary, Rosaleen and Wendy are

A. ☐ Rose's cousins.

B. ☐ Rose's new classmates.

C. ☐ Richard's old friends.

---

13. The young, tall girl with short curly hair is

A. ☐ Wendy.

B. ☐ Rosaleen.

C. ☐ Mary.

---

14. Mary is the girl

A. ☐ with long dark hair and blue eyes.

B. ☐ with long dark hair and green eyes.

C. ☐ with short blonde hair and brown eyes.

---

15. Rosaleen is

A. ☐ very patient and hardworking.

B. ☐ very friendly and fashionable.

C. ☐ very fashionable and patient.

Part 4 | Questions 16 – 20

Ascolterai una persona raccontare ad una sua amica la sua vacanza ad Ischia. Dopo aver ascoltato attentamente, scrivi la parola mancante in ciascuno spazio. Scrivi solo UNA parola per ciascuno spazio. La conversazione verrà ripetuta due volte. Ti viene fornito un esempio (**0**) *all'inizio del testo.*

A trip to Ischia

Location: A small island, called (**0**) ....Ischia.........., off the coast of Naples.

Mean of transport: (**16**) .... boat.

Number of days spent in Ischia: (**17**) .... days.

Cost: € (**18**) ....

Accomodation: Hotel or (**19**) ....

Organisers: Global Travel Club of (**20**) ....

Part 5 | Questions 21 – 25

Ascolterai una presentatrice che illustra una festa locale. Dopo aver ascoltato attentamente, scrivi la parola mancante in ciascuno spazio per completare la scheda. Scrivi solo UNA parola per ciascuno spazio. L'annuncio verrà ripetuto due volte. Ti viene fornito un esempio (**0**) *all'inizio del testo.*

Pizza party!

Date: Sunday (**0**) ....14th.......... of June.

When? From 6 pm on Sunday to (**21**) .... pm on Monday.

Tickets: £ (**22**) .... per person.

Special discount price: children under the age of (**23**) .... go in for £2!

Contact person: Tracey (**24**) ....

Phone: call Tracey on (**25**) .... to book tickets!

LISTENING TEST 6

Part 1 | Questions 1 – 5

*Ascolterai cinque brevi conversazioni, ciascuna delle quali verrà ripetuta due volte. Dopo aver ascoltato attentamente, rispondi al quesito relativo a ciascuna conversazione scegliendo la risposta corretta (**A**, **B** oppure **C**) in base a ciò che hai ascoltato. Prima di cominciare, ti viene fornito un esempio (**0**).*

Example

0 What will the speakers buy Jacqueline?

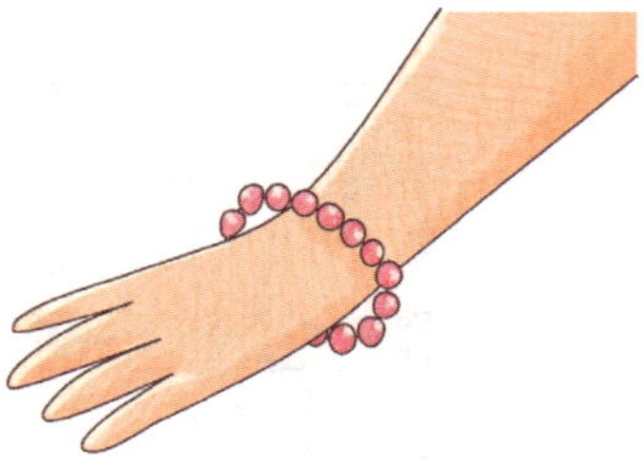
A. ☐

B. ☒

C. ☐

---

1. What will Chris get for his birthday?

A. ☐

B. ☐

C. ☐

2. What does Mr Haffman look like?

A. ☐

B. ☐

C. ☐

3. Where is the man going to plant the tree?

A. ☐

B. ☐

C. ☐

4. Where is the mop and bucket?

A. ☐

B. ☐

C. ☐

5. What has John got?

A. ☐

B. ☐

C. ☐

Part 2 | Questions 6 – 10

27 *Ascolterai Jenny parlare col suo amico Alex della sua vacanza in Italia. Cosa ha fatto in vacanza ciascuna persona? Dopo aver ascoltato attentamente, scrivi accanto al nome di ciascun partecipante* (**6 – 10**) *l'attività svolta* (**A – H**). *La conversazione verrà ripetuta due volte. Ti viene fornito un esempio* (**0**) *all'inizio.*

Example

0 ☐F Frank

People

6. ☐ Jenny
7. ☐ dad
8. ☐ brother
9. ☐ sister
10. ☐ mum

Activities

A. reading
B. windsurfing
C. shopping
D. taking photos
E. sightseeing
F. swimming
G. go-karting
H. snorkelling

Part 3 | Questions 11 – 15

*Ascolterai una coppia di amiche, Marylin e Jessica, prendere accordi per andare insieme ad un nuovo ristorante. Dopo aver ascoltato attentamente, rispondi a ciascun quesito scegliendo la risposta corretta (***A**, **B** *oppure* **C***) in base a ciò che hai ascoltato. La conversazione verrà ripetuta due volte. Ti viene fornito un esempio* **(0)** *all'inizio.*

Example

0

The new restaurant serves

A. ☐ Mexican food.

B. ☐ Italian food.

C. ☒ Greek food.

11. The restaurant opened

A. ☐ three weeks ago
B. ☐ two weeks ago.
C. ☐ one week ago.

---

12. The food was

A. ☐ really tasty.
B. ☐ tasty.
C. ☐ not so tasty, especially the pizza.

---

13. Eva

A. ☐ had a problem with the dessert.
B. ☐ said that the pasta was great.
C. ☐ found the pizza very tasty.

---

14. After the meal, Jessica went

A. ☐ to the doctor's.
B. ☐ to the café with Eva.
C. ☐ to her house.

---

15. In the end, they spent

A. ☐ £20.
B. ☐ £40.
C. ☐ £50.

Part 4 | Questions 16 – 20

*Ascolterai Max chiedere alcune informazioni a Sarah in vista di una prossima vacanza a Manchester. Dopo aver ascoltato attentamente, scrivi la parola mancante in ciascuno spazio. Scrivi solo UNA parola per ciascuno spazio. La conversazione verrà ripetuta due volte. Ti viene fornito un esempio (**0**) all'inizio del testo.*

My trip to Manchester!

When: (**0**) October

Temperature in autumn about: (**16**) .... degrees.

Will need to wear: (**17**) ....

Name of the train station in London: € (**18**) ....

Cost of train: € (**19**) ....

Take Sarah some: (**20**) ....

Part 5 | Questions 21 – 25

*Ascolterai un messaggio pubblicitario che presenta un nuovo ristorante. Dopo aver ascoltato attentamente, scrivi la parola mancante in ciascuno spazio per completare la scheda. Scrivi solo UNA parola per ciascuno spazio. L'annuncio verrà ripetuto due volte. Ti viene fornito un esempio (**0**) all'inizio del testo.*

A new restaurant

Name: (**0**) IndiaForYou 72 Green Street.

Ground floor: (**21**) .... and dinner for families with children.

Top floor: Suitable for (**22**) .... parties.

Open from (**23**) .... to Sunday.

You can get more (**24**) .... dishes, made especially for you.

Garden: (**25**) .... tables for anybody to sit at.

1 Il plurale dei nomi

- Il **plurale dei nomi** si ottiene aggiungendo **-s** al nome singolare: *book* → *books*.

  - Se il nome singolare termina in **-s**, **-ss**, **-sh**, **-ch**, **-x**, **-o**, **-z**, si aggiunge **-es**: *bus* → *buses*.
  - Alcuni nomi terminanti in **-o**, tuttavia, aggiungono solo la **-s**: *discos*, *photos*, *pianos*, *videos*, *radios*.
  - Se il nome singolare termina con consonante + **-y**, si toglie la **-y** e si aggiunge **-ies**: *country* → *countries*.
  - Se il nome singolare termina con **-f** o **-fe**, questi si tolgono e si aggiunge **-ves**: *shelf* → *shelves*; *life* → *lives*.

- Alcuni plurali sono irregolari:

child → *children*	*man* → *men*
tooth → *teeth*	*person* → *people*
woman → *women*	*foot* → *feet*
mouse → *mice*	

- In alcuni casi invece il plurale è uguale al singolare:

one fish → *two fish*	*one sheep* → *two sheep*

2 Le *question words*

- Le ***question words*** si usano per formulare domande. Si collocano sempre all'inizio della frase interrogativa.
  Who is your English teacher? = Chi è il tuo / vostro insegnante di inglese?
  What's your name? = Qual è il tuo nome? / Come ti chiami?
  When is your birthday? = Quand'è il tuo compleanno?
  How are you? = Come stai?
  How old are you? = Quanti anni hai?
- Le eventuali preposizioni vanno alla fine della frase:
  *Where are you **from**?* = Di dove sei?
- ***What*** e ***which*** significano entrambi "quale", ma ***which*** si usa per indicare **una scelta tra due o più opzioni**:
  What are your favourite books? = Quali sono i tuoi libri preferiti?
  Which is your first language, English or Italian? = Qual è la tua prima lingua, l'inglese o l'italiano?

3 Il genitivo sassone e *whose*

- In inglese il possesso o il rapporto tra persone si esprime con il nome del **possessore** + **'s** + **nome della cosa** o della persona, senza l'articolo:
  It's Sue's birthday. = È il compleanno di Sue.
  She's Becky's mum. = È la mamma di Becky.
- Quando due persone possiedono qualcosa insieme s aggiunge ***'s*** alla seconda persona:
  This is Alex and Jamie's room. = Questa è la stanza di Alex e Jamie.
- Ai nomi che terminano in **-s** e ai plurali regolari si aggiunge solo l'apostrofo:
  Clara is Janis' cousin. = Clara è la cugina di Janis.
  This is the girls' room. = Questa è la camera delle ragazz

> **Attenzione !**
> La s preceduta dall'apostrofo ('s) può essere:
> - ***is***, terza persona singolare di *be*: *Anne's happy.* = Anne è felice.
> - ***has***, terza persona singolare di *have got*: *Anne's got two sisters.* = Anne ha due sorelle.
> - la ***'s*** che esprime possesso: *This is Anne's mobile phone.* = Questo è il cellulare di Anne.

- ***Whose*** significa "Di chi?" ed è usato come aggettivo o come pronome. Si possono avere due costruzioni: *Whose pen is it?* oppure *Whose is this pen?* = Di chi è questa penna?

4 *Present simple*

- Il ***Present simple*** si ottiene con la forma base del verbo, cioè la forma che trovi sul dizionario (infinito senza *to*). Alla terza persona singolare (*he* / *she* / *it*) si aggiunge **-s** alla forma base.
- Il ***Present simple*** si usa per parlare di azioni abituali, di attività frequenti, di situazioni permanenti e di fatti che sono sempre veri:
  I get up at 7 o'clock. = Mi alzo alle sette in punto.
  They live in Spain. = Vivono in Spagna.
  Water boils at 100°C. = L'acqua bolle a 100°C.
- La **forma negativa** si ottiene con: **soggetto** + ***do*** / ***does*** + ***not*** + **forma base** (forma estesa) o **soggetto** + ***don't*** / ***doesn't*** + **forma base** (forma contratta). La forma contratta è la più usata nell'inglese parlato e in quello scritto informale:
  Terry doesn't play volleyball. = Terry non gioca a pallavolo
- La struttura delle **frasi interrogative** è: ***do*** / ***does*** + **soggetto** + **forma base del verbo** + **?**

- La struttura delle **risposte brevi** è: ***Yes***, + **pronome soggetto** + ***do*** / ***does***; ***No***, + **pronome soggetto** + ***don't*** / ***doesn't***:
  'Do they watch TV at night?' 'No, they don't.' = "Guardano la TV di sera?" "No."

-ch, -sh, -ss, -x, -zz, -o	*-es*
watch	watch**es**
wash	wash**es**
kiss	kiss**es**
relax	relax**es**
buzz	buzz**es**
do	do**es**

consonante + *-y*	*-ies*
study	stud**ies**
vocale + *-y*	***-s***
play	play**s**

Attenzione !
Il verbo ***do*** viene usato sia come ausiliare per ottenere la forma negativa, interrogativa e le risposte brevi del *Present simple*, sia come un normale verbo che significa "fare":
I do sport every day. = Faccio sport tutti i giorni.
Jenny doesn't do sport. = Jenny non fa sport.
Do you do sport every day? = Fai / Fate sport tutti i giorni?

5 *like, love, hate + -ing*

- In inglese il verbo ***like***, (piacere), ha una costruzione particolare, diversa da quella italiana: **soggetto** (la persona a cui piace qualcosa) + ***like*** + **oggetto** (ciò che piace):
  I like pizza. = Mi piace la pizza.
  Jeff doesn't like musicals. = A Jeff non piacciono i musical.
- I verbi ***like*** (piacere), ***love*** (amare), ***hate*** (odiare), ***enjoy*** (divertirsi, godersi qualcosa) sono seguiti dalla forma in ***-ing*** del verbo:
  I like playing tennis. = Mi piace giocare a tennis.
  They hate cleaning their room. = Odiano pulire la loro stanza.

Forma base	Forma in *-ing*
eat	eat**ing**
pla**y**	play**ing**
stud**y**	study**ing**
hav**e**	hav**ing**
sto**p**	stop**ping**
li**e**	ly**ing**

6 I nomi numerabili e non numerabili

- Sono numerabili (***countable***) i nomi di cose, animali e persone che si possono contare e che hanno forma plurale: *eggs*, *biscuits*, *oranges*, ecc.
- Sono non numerabili (***uncountable***) i nomi di cose che non si possono contare e che hanno solo la forma singolare: *sugar*, *water*, *bread*, ecc.
- Non si può mai usare l'articolo indeterminativo (*a* / *an*) davanti ai sostantivi non numerabili. Per indicare una quantità precisa con i sostantivi non numerabili bisogna usare altre espressioni:
  - *a glass of water* = un bicchiere d'acqua
  - *a packet of sugar* = un pacchetto di zucchero
  - *a piece / a slice of bread* = un pezzo / una fetta di pane
  - *a cup of coffee / tea* = una tazza di caffè / tè
  - *a bottle of water / milk* = una bottiglia d'acqua / di latte

7 Gli avverbi di frequenza

- Si usano per indicare con quale frequenza viene compiuta un'azione. L'avverbio di frequenza segue il verbo *be*, ma precede gli altri verbi:
  You are always late for school. = Sei sempre in ritardo per la scuola.
  We often go to the cinema. = Andiamo spesso al cinema.

8 *some / any*

- Si usano ***some*** e ***any*** per indicare una quantità non definita, sia con nomi numerabili plurali (libri, biscotti, amici) sia con nomi non numerabili (latte, pasta, caffè). Corrispondono all'italiano "un po', alcuni, qualche, del, della, dei, degli, delle".
- Nelle frasi affermative si usa ***some***:
  There is some milk. = C'è del latte.
  I've got some comics. = Ho dei fumetti.
- Nelle frasi negative e nelle domande si usa ***any***:
  She hasn't got any dolls. = Non ha bambole.
  Is there any dessert? = C'è del dolce?

9 How much? / How many?

- ***How much*** e ***How many*** si usano per informarsi sulla quantità di qualcosa.
- ***How much*** (quanto, quanta) si usa con i sostantivi non numerabili e per chiedere il prezzo di qualcosa:
  How much ice cream is there? = Quanto gelato c'è?
  How much are the pizzas? = Quanto costano / vengono le pizze?
- ***How many*** (quanti, quante) si usa con i sostantivi numerabili plurali:
  How many posters have you got in your room? = Quanti poster hai nella tua stanza / in camera tua?

10 Il verbo modale *can / can't*

- Il verbo ***can*** significa potere, saper (fare), riuscire, e si usa, tra le altre cose, per esprimere l'abilità, la capacità di fare qualcosa. È un verbo modale ed è uguale per tutte le persone.
  È sempre seguito dalla forma base del verbo principale:
  I can sing. = So cantare.
- Per la **forma negativa** si aggiunge ***not***:
  I can't play the guitar. = Non so suonare la chitarra.
- La struttura delle **frasi interrogative** è: ***Can*** + **soggetto** + **forma base del verbo**.
- La struttura delle **risposte brevi** è: ***Yes,*** + **pronome soggetto** + ***can.*** / ***No,*** + **pronome soggetto** + ***can't***:
  'Can you speak French?' 'Yes, I can.' / 'No, I can't.' = "Parli / Sai parlare il francese?" "Sì." / "No."

11 Present continuous

- Il ***Present continuous*** si usa per indicare azioni che si stanno svolgendo nel momento in cui si parla, o per due azioni che si svolgono contemporaneamente.
- È spesso accompagnato da espressioni di tempo come ***now*** (adesso, ora), ***at the moment*** (in questo momento), ***today*** (oggi).
- La **forma affermativa** si ottiene con: **soggetto** + ***am*** / ***are*** / ***is*** + **forma in *-ing*** del verbo:
  I am wearing jeans at the moment. = Sto indossando / Indosso i jeans in questo momento.
  It's raining today. = Oggi piove.
- La **forma negativa** si ottiene con: **soggetto** + ***am*** / ***are*** / ***is*** + ***not*** + **forma in *-ing*** del verbo:
  It isn't snowing at the moment. = Non nevica in questo momento.
- La **forma interrogativa** si ottiene con: ***am*** / ***are*** / ***is*** + **soggetto** + **forma in *-ing*** del verbo + **?**
- Le **risposte brevi** sono identiche alle risposte brevi del presente di *be*:
  'Are they doing their homework?' 'Yes, they are.' / 'No, they aren't.' = "Fanno / Stanno facendo i compiti?" "Sì." "No."

In italiano il *Present continuous* si traduce con il verbo "stare" seguito dal gerundio, ma anche con il presente indicativo.

- Il *Present continuous* NON si usa con i seguenti verbi: *hear, see, love, like, want, believe, know*.

12 Il *Past simple* di *be* + espressioni di tempo passato

- Il ***Past simple*** di *be* ha due voci: ***was*** per la prima e la terza persona singolari, ***were*** per la seconda persona singolare e per le persone plurali. In italiano può corrispondere al passato remoto, al passato prossimo oppure all'imperfetto. Si usa per indicare azioni o situazioni accadute in un determinato tempo del passato e concluse.
- Spesso è accompagnato da **espressioni di tempo al passato** come *yesterday, last night / week / month / year, a month / year / three days ago, in 1955, when I was a child…*
  We were at the seaside last month. = Eravamo al mare il mese scorso.
  This house was built in 1980. = Questa casa è stata costruita nel 1980.
  They were here a month ago. = Erano qui un mese fa.
- Le **forme negativa** e **interrogativa** e le **risposte brevi** seguono le stesse regole di formazione del verbo *be* al *Present simple*:
  Where were you yesterday morning? = Dov'eri ieri mattina?
  'Was she blonde when she was a child?' 'Yes, she was!' = "Era bionda da bambina?" "Sì!"

13 *Past simple*

- Il ***Past simple*** si usa per parlare di azioni ed eventi completamente conclusi nel passato. Il ***Past simple*** dei verbi regolari si ottiene aggiungendo ***-ed*** alla forma base del verbo ed è uguale per tutte le persone. Alcuni verbi subiscono delle variazioni ortografiche.
I played volleyball yesterday. = Ieri ho giocato a pallavolo.
- I **verbi irregolari** non aggiungono ***-ed*** ma hanno una forma propria che va imparata a memoria (vedi la tabella a pag. 208). Anche per i verbi irregolari il ***Past simple*** è uguale per tutte le persone, fatta eccezione per il verbo ***be***.
They ate a lot last night. = Hanno mangiato molto ieri sera.
- Per le **forme interrogativa** e **negativa** e per le **risposte brevi** si deve usare l'ausiliare ***did*** / ***didn't***.

Attenzione !
Ricorda che in presenza di un ausiliare il verbo principale resta sempre alla forma base!

She didn't play basketball three years ago. = Non giocava a basket tre anni fa.
Did your sister like the present? = A tua sorella è piaciuto il regalo?
Yes, she did. / No, she didn't. = Sì. / No.
What did you do yesterday afternoon? = Cosa hai fatto ieri pomeriggio?

14 Il verbo modale *could / couldn't*

- ***Could*** è il passato e il condizionale di ***can*** e si usa per:
  - indicare abilità o inabilità nel passato:
  They couldn't book a table at the restaurant. = Non riuscirono a prenotare un tavolo al ristorante.
  - indicare la possibilità o l'impossibilità di fare qualcosa al passato:
  I couldn't call you yesterday. My phone wasn't working. = Non ti ho potuto chiamare ieri. Il mio telefono non funzionava.
  - fare una richiesta in modo formale e cortese:
  Could you repeat the instructions, please? = Può ripetere le istruzioni, per piacere?
  - esprimere un suggerimento:
  You could do more exercise. = Potresti fare più movimento.

15 I pronomi relativi *who, which, that*

- ***Who***, ***which*** e ***that*** sono pronomi relativi (***relative pronouns***) che mettono in relazione due proposizioni, quella reggente e quella subordinata relativa, in cui vengono aggiunte ulteriori informazioni su un sostantivo o un pronome nominato nella reggente.
- Sono invariabili in genere e numero: ***who*** (oppure ***that***) si usa per le persone; ***which*** (oppure ***that***) si usa per animali e oggetti.
- Quando il pronome relativo è il **soggetto** della frase relativa **deve sempre essere espresso**. Quando il pronome relativo è complemento oggetto può essere omesso:
*The boy **who / that** is talking to Nick is my friend.* = Il ragazzo **che** sta parlando con Nick è un mio amico. (soggetto)
*This is the film **which / that** won a special award in 2016.* = Questo è il film **che** ha vinto un premio speciale nel 2016. (soggetto)
*She's the girl (**who / that**) I met at Leo's party.* = È la ragazza che ho incontrato alla festa di Leo. (oggetto)
*Show me the photos (**which / that**) you took in Paris.* = Fammi vedere le foto che hai fatto a Parigi. (oggetto)

A differenza dell'inglese, in italiano questi pronomi relativi possono essere espressi da "che" (invariabile in genere e numero) oppure da "il quale, la quale, i quali, le quali" che invece si accordano in genere e numero. Non c'è differenza tra persone, animali e oggetti.

16 Il comparativo degli aggettivi

- Per confrontare due persone, cose o categorie si usa il comparativo di un aggettivo + ***than*** che introduce il secondo termine di paragone.
- Gli aggettivi brevi aggiungono ***-er***:
Colin is shorter than his brother. = Colin è più basso di suo fratello.
- Osserva le variazioni ortografiche:
  - se l'aggettivo termina con **una vocale** + **una consonante** si raddoppia la consonante:
  fat → *fatter*
  - se termina per ***-e*** muta si aggiunge soltanto ***-r***:
  large → *larger*
  - se termina in ***-y*** preceduta da consonante si toglie la ***-y*** e si aggiunge ***-ier***: *easy* → *easier*

- Gli aggettivi lunghi sono preceduti da ***more***:
Maths tests are more difficult than English tests. = Le verifiche di matematica sono più difficili di quelle di inglese.

Attenzione !
Alcuni comparativi sono irregolari:
good / well → better; bad → worse; far → further / farther.

17 Il superlativo degli aggettivi

- Si usa il **superlativo relativo** di un aggettivo per paragonare una cosa o persona con tutte le altre cose o persone in quel gruppo. Gli aggettivi brevi aggiungono ***-est***:
Jamie is the shortest in his class. = Jamie è il più basso della classe.

- Osserva le variazioni ortografiche:
  - se l'aggettivo termina con **una vocale** + **una consonante** si raddoppia la consonante: *fat → the fat**test***
  - se termina per ***-e*** muta si aggiunge soltanto ***-st***: *large → the larg**est***
  - se termina in ***-y*** preceduta da consonante si toglie la ***-y*** e si aggiunge ***-iest***: *easy → the eas**iest***.

- Gli aggettivi lunghi sono preceduti da ***the most***:
Chemistry tests are the most difficult. = Le verifiche di chimica sono le più difficili.

Attenzione !
Alcuni superlativi sono irregolari:
good / well → the best; bad → the worst; far → the furthest / farthest.

- L'aggettivo al grado superlativo è sempre preceduto dall'articolo ***the*** e può essere seguito da ***in*** + **luogo** o gruppo di persone oppure da ***of*** + **nome** o pronome plurale.

18 Il comparativo di uguaglianza: *(not) as … as*

- Il comparativo di uguaglianza si forma con (***not***) ***as*** + **aggettivo** + ***as***. Si usa per dire che due cose, animali o persone hanno o non hanno la stessa qualità:
I'm as tall as my sister. = Sono alto quanto mia sorella.

19 *have to / don't have to*

- Si usa ***have to*** + **forma base** del verbo per esprimere un dovere o un obbligo imposto da qualcun altro. ***Have to*** non è un verbo modale, ha tutti i tempi e i modi e si usa anche per coniugare ***must***, "dovere", nei tempi mancanti. Il verbo ***have to*** costruisce le forme negativa e interrogativa e le risposte brevi con l'ausiliare ***do***:
You have to wear a uniform in this school. = Dovete indossare la divisa in questa scuola.
'Did you have to wear a uniform at primary school?' 'Yes, I did./ No, I didn't.' = "Dovevi indossare una divisa alle scuole elementari?" "Sì. / No."

Attenzione !
La **forma negativa** (***don't have to*** + forma base del verbo) si usa per indicare che non è necessario o non è obbligatorio fare qualcosa:
I don't have to go to school on Sundays. = Non devo andare a scuola di sabato.

20 *must / mustn't*

- Il verbo ***must*** è un verbo modale, perciò è uguale per tutte le persone, è sempre seguito dalla forma base del verbo principale e usa solo ***not*** (***n't***) per la forma negativa. Si usa ***must*** per dare un ordine o esprimere un dovere, un obbligo, spesso avvertito dal soggetto stesso:
I can't come with you. I must study. = Non posso venire con te. Devo studiare.

- Si usa ***mustn't*** per esprimere una proibizione o un divieto:
You mustn't run in the corridor. = Non dovete correre nel corridoio.

Attenzione !
Must e ***mustn't*** si usano soltanto al presente. Per costruire i tempi mancanti del verbo "dovere" si usa ***have to***.

21 *be going to*

- Il futuro con ***be going to*** si ottiene con il presente del verbo *be* seguito da *going to* e dalla forma base del verbo principale. Si usa:
  - per esprimere l'intenzione di fare qualcosa nel futuro:
  She's going to have a party next week. = Darà / Ha intenzione di dare una festa la settimana prossima.
  What are you going to do after the university? = Che farai dopo l'università?

- per fare previsioni sulla base di ciò che vediamo o per indicare un evento che sta per accadere:
  Look at the sky. It's going to snow. = Guarda il cielo. Sta per nevicare. / Nevicherà.

22 Past participle

- Il ***Past participle*** dei verbi regolari segue le stesse regole di formazione del *Past simple*: si aggiunge ***-ed*** alla forma base del verbo. Il ***Past participle*** dei verbi irregolari varia. (vedi pag. 208)

23 Present perfect

- Il ***Present perfect*** si forma con **soggetto** + ***have*** / ***has*** + ***Past participle*** del verbo principale. Per la forma negativa si aggiunge ***not*** dopo il verbo ausiliare. Nella forma interrogativa il verbo ausiliare precede il soggetto.
- Il ***Present perfect*** si usa per parlare di azioni avvenute in un tempo non precisato del passato: l'attenzione è posta sull'azione e i suoi effetti sul presente, non su quando è avvenuta:
  The film has ended. = Il film è finito.
  The teacher hasn't given any homework. = L'insegnante non ha dato compiti.
  Have you seen my sweatshirt? = Hai visto la mia felpa?
- Si usa anche per indicare azioni avvenute in un passato recente oppure in un periodo di tempo non ancora concluso. In questi casi è spesso accompagnato da espressioni di tempo come *recently, today, this morning / week / month / year…* che di solito si trovano alla fine della frase:
  I haven't heard the news today. = Non ho sentito le notizie oggi.

Attenzione!
Come participio passato di ***go*** si usa ***gone*** per indicare che qualcuno è andato in un luogo e non è ancora tornato, ***been*** per indicare che quella persona è stata in un luogo ed è tornata:
Lisa has gone to the gym. = Lisa è andata in palestra. (non è ancora tornata)
Lisa has been to the gym. = Lisa è andata / stata in palestra. (è tornata)

24 Present perfect with ever and never

- Gli avverbi ***ever*** (nelle frasi interrogative) e ***never*** (nelle frasi negative, lasciando il verbo affermativo) si usano con il ***Present perfect*** per parlare di azioni mai fatte prima:
  Have you ever listened to classical music? = Hai mai ascoltato musica classica?
  They've never studied Russian. = Non hanno mai studiato il russo.

Ricorda!
Questi avverbi si trovano sempre prima del participio passato.

25 Present perfect with for, since and how long

- Il ***Present perfect*** si usa anche per descrivere un'azione iniziata nel passato e che continua nel presente (forma di durata).
- Per indicare il **momento iniziale** dell'azione si usa ***since***:
  She has lived in this house since she was a child / 2015 / last summer. = Vive in questa casa da quando era bambina / dal 2015 / dall'estate scorsa.
- Per indicare la **durata** dell'azione si usa ***for***:
  I've been here for an hour/ three years / a long time. = Sono qui da un'ora / tre anni / tanto tempo.
- Per chiedere **da quanto tempo** è iniziata un'azione si usa ***How long***. ***How long*** può significare "da quando" oppure "da quanto tempo":
  How long have you been here? = Da quando / Da quanto tempo sei qui?

In italiano la forma di durata si traduce con il **presente indicativo**. Sia ***for*** che ***since*** significano "da".

26 Present perfect or Past simple?

- Si usa il ***Past simple*** per parlare di azioni ed eventi conclusi in un tempo determinato del passato o che non hanno nessun legame con il presente. È accompagnato da espressioni di tempo come ***yesterday***, ***two days ago***, ***last month*** / ***year***. Per la formazione, ricorda che i verbi possono essere regolari e irregolari. (Per la lista dei verbi irregolari, vai alla pagina 208.)

- Per le **forme negativa** e **interrogativa** usiamo l'ausiliare ***did*** seguito dalla forma base del verbo principale:
I saw her yesterday. = L'ho vista ieri.
When did you see her? = Quando l'hai vista?
I didn't see her yesterday. = Non l'ho vista ieri.
- Si usa il ***Present perfect*** per parlare di azioni terminate da poco e per esprimere il risultato presente di un'azione passata (con ***just***, ***already***, ***yet***):
*I've **just** seen her.* = L'ho appena vista.
- Si usa anche per descrivere avvenimenti ed esperienze senza un riferimento preciso di tempo o che non sono mai avvenuti (con ***ever*** e ***never***).
I've never run a marathon! = Non ho mai corso una maratona!
- Si usa inoltre per azioni avvenute in un tempo passato non ancora concluso:
I've read five books this month. = Ho letto cinque libri questo mese.
- Anche la **forma di durata** si esprime con il ***Present perfect***, accompagnato da ***for*** e ***since*** e dalle domande con ***How long…?***:
They've lived in France for ten years. = Vivono in Francia da dieci anni.
- Ricorda che anche il participio passato dei verbi irregolari cambia (vedi pag. 208)

27 Il futuro con *will*

- Il futuro con ***will*** (***Future simple***) si usa per fare previsioni sul futuro, per fare promesse e con i verbi di opinione ***think***, ***know***, ***believe***, ***hope***:
I promise I'll come to your party. = Prometto che verrò alla tua festa.
We think we'll go to the cinema on Saturday. = Pensiamo di andare al cinema sabato.
- La **forma affermativa** e quella **negativa** si ottengono con **soggetto** + ***will*** (***'ll***) / ***will not*** (***won't***) + **forma base** del verbo:
It won't snow a lot this winter. = Non nevicherà molto questo inverno.
- La **forma interrogativa** si ottiene con ***will*** + **soggetto** + **forma base** del verbo + ...?:
Will they reply to my request? = Risponderanno alla mia richiesta?
- Per la prima persona singolare e plurale si può usare anche l'ausiliare ***shall***, ma nell'inglese parlato e informale si usa ***will*** per tutte le persone, di solito alla forma contratta ***'ll***.

28 *be going to* o *will*?

- Si usa il futuro con ***be going to*** seguito dalla forma base del verbo principale per esprimere l'intenzione di fare qualcosa:
I'm going to study abroad. = Studierò / Ho intenzione di studiare all'estero.
- Si usa ***be going to*** anche per indicare qualcosa che sta per succedere:
Look at those clouds. It's going to rain. = Guarda quelle nubi. Sta per piovere. / Pioverà.
- Si usa il futuro con ***will*** / ***won't*** seguito dal verbo principale per parlare di previsioni future, per esprimere un'opinione e per fare promesse:
The future of the planet will depend on our choices. = Il futuro del pianeta dipenderà dalle nostre scelte.
I think they will sell the house. = Penso che venderanno la casa.
I'll come to the match. = Verrò alla partita.
- ***will*** / ***won't*** si usa inoltre nel periodo ipotetico di tipo 1:
We'll stay at home if it rains. = Resteremo a casa se pioverà.

29 *Zero conditional*

- Lo ***Zero conditional***, o periodo ipotetico generale, si usa per regole generali o leggi scientifiche. Ha due parti: la proposizione principale (***main clause***) che esprime la conseguenza e quella subordinata, introdotta da ***if*** o ***when***, che esprime l'ipotesi. La proposizione subordinata può precedere o seguire quella principale. Il tempo verbale è il ***Present simple*** sia nella ***if clause*** che nella ***main clause***:
***If** you touch a fire, you get burned.* = Se tocchi il fuoco, ti bruci.
*Ice melts **when** you heat it.* = Il ghiaccio si scioglie quando lo scaldi.
- Lo ***Zero conditional*** si usa anche per dare consigli o comandi; in questo caso nella *main clause* si usa l'imperativo:
If you drink, don't drive! = Se bevi, non guidare!

30 *First conditional*

- Il ***First conditional*** (periodo ipotetico di tipo 1) indica la **possibilità** o la **probabilità** che una situazione si verifichi nel futuro e si usa per predire possibili azioni o conseguenze future e per dare consigli:
Will they come to our party ***if*** *we invite them?* = Verranno alla nostra festa se li inviteremo?
When *I have time, I'll cut the grass.* = Quando avrò tempo taglierò l'erba.

In inglese il verbo della proposizione principale è sempre al futuro con *will*, mentre quello della subordinata è sempre al *Present simple*. In italiano invece il verbo della proposizione subordinata può essere sia al presente indicativo, sia al futuro (doppio futuro).

31 *Second conditional*

- Usiamo il ***Second conditional*** per parlare di situazioni improbabili o immaginarie. La frase subordinata è introdotta da ***if***, mentre il tempo verbale è al *Past simple*; nella frase principale si usa ***would*** (***'d***), seguito dalla forma base del verbo:
If *I read that book, I* ***would*** *know the answer.* = Se avessi letto quel libro, saprei la risposta.

32 *may e might*

- ***May*** e ***might*** si usano per esprimere una possibilità presente o futura e per fare previsioni:
The weather forecast says it may/might snow tomorrow. = Le previsioni del tempo dicono che potrebbe nevicare domani.
- La **forma affermativa** si ottiene con **soggetto** + ***may/might*** + **forma base** del verbo: *Kath may/might join us later.* = Kath potrebbe raggiungerci più tardi.
- La **forma negativa** si ottiene con **soggetto** + ***may/ might not*** + **forma base** del verbo: *Kath may/might not join us.* = Kath potrebbe non raggiungerci.

Attenzione!
Non esiste la forma negativa contratta di *may*.

Le frasi con ***may/might*** possono essere tradotte in italiano in diversi modi:
They may/might come later. = Potrebbero arrivare più tardi. / Può darsi che arrivino più tardi. / Forse arriveranno più tardi.

33 Composti di *some, any, no, every*

- Con ***some***, ***any***, ***no*** ed ***every*** si possono costruire pronomi e avverbi indefiniti che si riferiscono alle persone, alle cose e ai luoghi. Gli indefiniti composti sono sempre seguiti da un verbo alla terza persona singolare.
- I composti di ***some*** si usano nelle frasi affermative:
Somebody / Someone is knocking at the door. = Qualcuno sta bussando alla porta.
- I composti di ***any*** si usano nelle frasi negative e nelle domande:
Is there anything to eat? = C'è qualcosa da mangiare?
There isn't anything on TV tonight. = Non c'è niente in TV stasera.

Attenzione!
Se la domanda è un'**offerta** oppure una **richiesta** si usano di solito i composti di ***some***:
Would you like / Can I have something to drink? = Vorresti / Posso avere qualcosa da bere?

- I composti di ***no*** si usano con il verbo alla forma affermativa:
Nobody went to the meeting. = Nessuno andò alla riunione.

34 *Need*

- Il verbo ***need*** significa "aver bisogno di" ed è un verbo regolare. Può essere seguito da un sostantivo o da ***to*** + **forma base** del verbo. È usato per esprimere necessità o mancanza di necessità:
I need a new pair of shoes. = Ho bisogno di un nuovo paio di scarpe.
They don't need to rush. = Non hanno bisogno / Non devono affrettarsi.

Attenzione!
Osserva la differenza:
You don't need to shout. (*need* è verbo) = Non devi / Non è necessario che tu urli.
There's no need to shout. (*need* è sostantivo) = Non c'è bisogno di urlare.

35 Il *Past continuous*

- Il ***Past continuous*** si forma con ***was*** / ***were*** + la forma in ***-ing*** del verbo principale. Le **forme interrogativa** e **negativa** e le **risposte brevi** seguono le regole di formazione del verbo *be* al *Past simple*. Si usa per descrivere azioni che erano in corso di svolgimento in un momento del passato:

In italiano il ***Past continuous*** si può tradurre con **l'imperfetto** oppure con il verbo **stare** + **gerundio**.

What were you doing this morning at 7? = Cosa facevi / stavi facendo alle 7 di questa mattina?
I was sleeping. = Dormivo / Stavo dormendo.

- Il ***Past continuous*** si usa spesso in una frase introdotta da ***while***, "mentre", quando due azioni sono simultanee:
They were talking ***while*** *she was cooking dinner.* = Parlavano mentre lei preparava la cena.

36 *Past continuous e Past simple con when e while*

- Il ***Past continuous*** può anche essere usato per indicare un'azione in corso di svolgimento nel passato che viene interrotta da un'altra, oppure un'azione in corso di svolgimento quando se ne verifica improvvisamente un'altra (al *Past simple*). Le due frasi sono di solito collegate da *while* seguito dal *Past continuous*, o da *when* seguito dal *Past simple*:
I was going to the library ***when*** *I met Susan.* = Stavo andando in biblioteca quando ho incontrato Susan.
While *I was drinking a coffee my mobile rang.* = Mentre bevevo un caffè, ha squillato il cellulare.

37 La forma passiva

- La **forma passiva** si usa quando si vuole mettere maggiormente in risalto l'azione rispetto a chi la compie.
- La forma passiva del ***Present simple*** si costruisce con **soggetto** + ***Present simple*** **del verbo** ***be*** + **participio passato** del verbo principale:
Royal Theatre tickets ***are sold*** *here.* = I biglietti del *Royal Theatre* sono venduti qui.
- Le forme negativa, interrogativa e le risposte brevi seguono le regole di formazione del verbo ***be***.
- La forma passiva del ***Past simple*** si costruisce con **soggetto** + ***Past simple*** **del verbo** ***be*** + **participio passato** del verbo principale:
The windows were cleaned yesterday. = Le finestre sono state pulite ieri.
- Le forme negativa, interrogativa e le risposte brevi seguono le regole di formazione del verbo ausiliare *be* al *Past simple*.

Attenzione !
Il **complemento d'agente** è sempre introdotto dalla preposizione ***by***:
The leaves are blown ***by*** *the wind.* = Le foglie sono mosse dal vento.

38 Il discorso diretto e indiretto

- Nel **discorso diretto** (***direct speech***) si riportano le parole esatte che vengono dette con una frase tra virgolette:
Billy says: 'Today it is cold.' = Billy dice: "Oggi fa freddo".
- Il **discorso indiretto** (***reported speech***) si usa invece quando riferiamo quello che qualcuno dice o ha detto:
Billy says (that) today it is cold. = Billy dice che oggi fa freddo.
- Il discorso indiretto è introdotto dai verbi ***say*** o ***tell***:
  - si usa ***say*** quando la persona a cui si parla non è indicata: *Jack says Rome is beautiful.* = Jack dice che Roma è bella.
  - si usa ***tell*** quando la persona a cui si parla è indicata: *Jack tells Brian Rome is beautiful.* = Jack dice a Brian che Roma è bella.
- Quando il verbo che introduce il discorso indiretto è al presente, nel passaggio dal discorso diretto a quello indiretto il tempo verbale non cambia. Negli altri casi i tempi verbali cambiano.
She says: 'I miss my friends'. = Lei disse: "Mi mancano i miei amici".
She says that she misses her friends. = Lei dice che le mancano i suoi amici.
- Nel passaggio da discorso diretto a indiretto anche i pronomi personali, gli aggettivi possessivi, i dimostrativi e le espressioni di tempo cambiano sempre:
*Ann said: '****This*** *is* ***my*** *bag'.* = Ann disse: "Questa è la mia borsa".
Ann said ***that*** *was* ***her*** *bag.* = Ann disse che quella era la sua borsa.

be – Present simple

Forma affermativa		Forma negativa	
Estesa	Contratta	Estesa	Contratta
I am	I'm	I am not	I'm not
you are	you're	you are not	you aren't
he / she / it is	he's / she's / it's	he / she / it is not	he / she / it isn't
we are	we're	we are not	we aren't
you are	you're	you are not	you aren't
they are	they're	they are not	they aren't

Forma interrogativa	Risposte brevi	
	Affermative	Negative
Am I... ?	Yes, you are.	No, you aren't.
Are you... ?	Yes, I am.	No, I'm not.
Is he / she / it... ?	Yes, he / she / it is.	No, he / she / it isn't.
Are we... ?	Yes, we are.	No, we aren't.
Are you... ?	Yes, you are.	No, you aren't.
Are they... ?	Yes, they are.	No, they aren't.

be – Past simple

Forma affermativa	Forma negativa	
	Estesa	Contratta
I was	I was not	I wasn't
you were	you were not	you weren't
he / she / it was	he / she / it was not	he / she / it wasn't
we were	we were not	we weren't
you were	you were not	you weren't
they were	they were not	they weren't

Forma interrogativa	Risposte brevi affermative	Risposte brevi negative
Was I... ?	Yes, you were.	No, you weren't.
Were you... ?	Yes, I was.	No, I wasn't.
Was he... / she... ? / it... ?	Yes, he / she / it was.	No, he / she / it wasn't.
Were we... ?	Yes, we were.	No, we weren't.
Were you... ?	Yes, you were.	No, you weren't.
Were they... ?	Yes, they were.	No, they weren't.

have got – Present simple

Forma affermativa		Forma negativa	
Estesa	Contratta	Estesa	Contratta
I have got	I've got	I have not got	I haven't got
you have got	you've got	you have not got	you haven't got
he / she / it has got	he's / she's / it's got	he / she / it has not got	he / she / it hasn't got
we have got	we've got	we have not got	we haven't got
you have got	you've got	you have not got	you haven't got
they have got	they've got	they have not got	they haven't got

Forma interrogativa	Risposte brevi	
	Affermative	Negative
Have I got…?	Yes, you have.	No, you haven't.
Have you got... ?	Yes, I have.	No, I haven't.
Has he / she / it got... ?	Yes, he / she / it has.	No, he / she / it hasn't.
Have we got... ?	Yes, we have.	No, we haven't.
Have you got... ?	Yes, you have.	No, you haven't.
Have they got... ?	Yes, they have.	No, they haven't.

Present simple

Forma affermativa	Forma negativa – Estesa	Forma negativa – Contratta
I live.	I do not live.	I don't live.
You live.	You do not live.	You don't live.
He / She / It lives.	He / She / It does not live.	He / She / It doesn't live.
We live.	We do not live.	We don't live.
You live.	You do not live.	You don't live.
They live.	They do not live.	They don't live.

Forma interrogativa	Risposte brevi – Affermative	Risposte brevi – Negative
Do I live…?	Yes, you do.	No, you don't.
Do you live…?	Yes, I do.	No, I don't.
Does he / she / it live…?	Yes, he / she / it does.	No, he / she / it doesn't.
Do we live…?	Yes, we do.	No, we don't.
Do you live…?	Yes, you do.	No, you don't.
Do they live…?	Yes, they do.	No, they don't.

Present continuous

Forma affermativa	Forma negativa – Estesa	Forma negativa – Contratta
I am walking.	I am not walking.	I'm not walking.
You are walking	You are not walking.	You aren't walking.
He / She / It is walking.	He / She / It is not walking.	He / She / It isn't walking.
We are walking.	We are not walking.	We aren't walking.
You are walking.	You are not walking.	You aren't walking.
They are walking.	They are not walking.	They aren't walking.

Forma interrogativa	Risposte brevi – Affermative	Risposte brevi – Negative
Am I walking?	Yes, you are.	No, you aren't.
Are you walking?	Yes, I am.	No, I'm not.
Is he / she / it walking?	Yes, he / she / it is.	No, he / she / it isn't.
Are we walking?	Yes, we are.	No, we aren't.
Are you walking?	Yes, you are.	No, you aren't.
Are they walking?	Yes, they are.	No, they aren't.

Spelling variations

Regole ortografiche per la formazione della terza persona singolare del *Present simple*.

-ch, -sh, -ss, -x, -zz, -o	watch	wash	kiss	relax	buzz	do
-es	watch**es**	wash**es**	kiss**es**	relax**es**	buzz**es**	do**es**

consonante + *-y*	study	vocale + *-y*	play
-ies	stud**ies**	*-s*	play**s**

Regole ortografiche per la forma in *-ing*.

Forma base	eat	pla**y**	stud**y**	hav**e**	sto**p**	**lie**
Forma in *-ing*	eat**ing**	play**ing**	study**ing**	hav**ing**	stop**ping**	**lying**

Past simple

Forma affermativa	Forma negativa	
	Estesa	Contratta
I walked. You walked. He / She / It walked. We walked. You walked. They walked.	I did not walk. You did not walk. He / She / It did not walk. We did not walk. You did not walk. They did not walk.	I didn't walk. You didn't walk. He / She / It didn't walk. We didn't walk. You didn't walk. They didn't walk.

Forma interrogativa	Risposte brevi	
	Affermative	Negative
Did I walk? Did you walk? Did he / she / it walk? Did we walk? Did you walk? Did they walk?	Yes, you did. Yes, I did. Yes, he / she / it did. Yes, we did. Yes, you did. Yes, they did.	No, you didn't. No, I didn't. No, he / she / it didn't. No, we didn't. No, you didn't. No, they didn't.

Present perfect

Forma affermativa		Forma negativa	
Estesa	Contratta	Estesa	Contratta
I have walked. You have walked. He / She / It has walked. We have walked. You have walked. They have walked.	I've walked. You've walked. He's / She's / It's walked. We've walked. You've walked. They've walked.	I have not walked. You have not walked. He / She / It has not walked. We have not walked. You have not walked. They have not walked.	I haven't walked. You haven't walked. He / She / It hasn't walked. We haven't walked. You haven't walked. They haven't walked.

Forma interrogativa	Risposte brevi	
	Affermative	Negative
Have I walked? Have you walked? Has he / she / it walked? Have we walked? Have you walked? Have they walked?	Yes, you have. Yes, I have. Yes, he / she / it has. Yes, we have. Yes, you have. Yes, they have.	No, you haven't. No, I haven't. No, he / she / it hasn't. No, we haven't. No, you haven't. No, they haven't.

be going to

Forma affermativa		Forma negativa	
Estesa	Contratta	Estesa	Contratta
I am going to walk. You are going to walk. He / She / It is going to walk. We are going to walk. You are going to walk. They are going to walk.	I'm going to walk. You're going to walk. He / She / It's going to walk. We're going to walk. You're going to walk. They're going to walk.	I am not going to walk. You are not going to walk. He / She / It is not going to walk. We are not going to walk. You are not going to walk. They are not going to walk.	I'm not going to walk. You aren't going to walk. He / She / It isn't going to walk. We aren't going to walk. You aren't going to walk. They aren't going to walk.

Forma interrogativa	Risposte brevi	
	Affermative	Negative
Am I going to walk...? Are you going to walk...? Is he / she / it going to walk...? Are we going to walk... ? Are you going to walk... ? Are they going to walk... ?	Yes, you are. Yes, I am. Yes, he / she / it is. Yes, we are. Yes, you are. Yes, they are.	No, you aren't. No, I'm not. No, he / she / it isn't. No, we aren't. No, you aren't. No, they aren't.

Irregular Verbs

Base form	Past simple	Past participle	In italiano
be	was, were	been	*essere*
become	became	become	*diventare*
begin	began	begun	*iniziare*
break	broke	broken	*rompere*
bring	brought	brought	*portare*
build	built	built	*costruire*
buy	bought	bought	*comprare*
catch	caught	caught	*prendere, afferrare*
choose	chose	chosen	*scegliere*
come	came	come	*venire*
cost	cost	cost	*costare*
cut	cut	cut	*tagliare*
do	did	done	*fare*
draw	drew	drawn	*disegnare*
dream	dreamed / dreamt	dreamed / dreamt	*sognare*
drive	drove	driven	*guidare*
drink	drank	drunk	*bere*
eat	ate	eaten	*mangiare*
fall	fell	fallen	*cadere*
feel	felt	felt	*sentire, provare*
fight	fought	fought	*combattere, litigare*
find	found	found	*trovare*
fly	flew	flown	*volare*
forget	forgot	forgotten	*dimenticare*
forgive	forgave	forgiven	*perdonare*
get	got	got / gotten	*ricevere, ottenere*
give	gave	given	*dare*
go	went	gone	*andare*
grow	grew	grown	*crescere*
have	had	had	*avere*
hear	heard	heard	*sentire, udire*
hit	hit	hit	*colpire*
keep	kept	kept	*tenere, mantenere*
know	knew	known	*sapere, conoscere*
learn	learned / learnt	learned / learnt	*imparare*
leave	left	left	*lasciare, partire*
lend	lent	lent	*prestare*
let	let	let	*permettere, lasciare*
lose	lost	lost	*perdere*
make	made	made	*fare, fabbricare*
mean	meant	meant	*significare, intendere*
meet	met	met	*incontrare, conoscere*
pay	paid	paid	*pagare*
put	put	put	*mettere*
read /ri:d/	read /red/	read /red/	*leggere*
ride	rode	ridden	*cavalcare*

Base form	Past simple	Past participle	In italiano
ring	rang	rung	*suonare, squillare*
run	ran	run	*correre*
say	said	said	*dire*
see	saw	seen	*vedere*
sell	sold	sold	*vendere*
send	sent	sent	*spedire, mandare*
show	showed	showed / shown	*mostrare*
shut	shut	shut	*chiudere*
sing	sang	sung	*cantare*
sit	sat	sat	*sedere*
sleep	slept	slept	*dormire*
speak	spoke	spoken	*parlare*
spend	spent	spent	*spendere, passare, trascorrere*
stand	stood	stood	*stare (in piedi)*
swim	swam	swum	*nuotare*
take	took	taken	*prendere*
teach	taught	taught	*insegnare*
tell	told	told	*dire, raccontare*
think	thought	thought	*pensare*
throw	threw	thrown	*gettare, buttare*
understand	understood	understood	*capire*
wake	woke	woken	*svegliarsi*
wear	wore	worn	*indossare*
win	won	won	*vincere*
write	wrote	written	*scrivere*